Studies in Celtic History VI

SAINT GERMANUS OF AUXERRE
AND THE END OF ROMAN BRITAIN

STUDIES IN CELTIC HISTORY
General editor David Dumville

SAINT GERMANUS OF AUXERRE AND THE END OF ROMAN BRITAIN

E. A. THOMPSON

THE BOYDELL PRESS

© E. A. Thompson 1984

First published 1984 by
The Boydell Press
an imprint of Boydell & Brewer Ltd
PO Box 9, Woodbridge, Suffolk IP12 3DF
and of Boydell & Brewer Inc.
Wolfeboro, New Hampshire 03894-2069, USA

Reprinted 1988

ISSN 0261 – 9865

British Library Cataloguing in Publication Data
Thompson, E.A.
  Saint Germanus of Auxerre and the end of
  Roman Britain.—(Studies in Celtic history,
  ISSN 0261-9865; v.6)
  1. Germanus, *Saint, Bishop of Auxerre*
  2. Great Britain—History—Roman period,
  55b.c.–449A.D.   3. Great Britain—
  Politics and government—To 1485
  I. Title   II. Series
  941.01'3   DA145.3.G4
  ISBN 0-85115-405-0

Library of Congress Cataloging-in-Publication Data
Thompson, E. A.
  Saint Germanus of Auxerre and the end of Roman Britain.
  (Studies in Celtic history ; 6)
  Bibliography: p.
  Includes index.
  1. Great Britain—History—Roman period, 55 B.C.—
449 A.D. 2. Constantius, of Lyons, fl. 480. Vita sancti
Germani. 3. Germanus, Saint, Bishop of Auxerre, 378–448.
4. Great Britain—Church history—To 449. I. Title.
II. Series.
DA145.T43 1984   936.1'03   84-18482
ISBN 0-85115-405-0

Printed and bound in Great Britain by
Billing & Sons Limited, Worcester

Contents

General Editor's Foreword

In this sixth volume of *Studies in Celtic History* we return to that ever compelling theme, the end of Roman Britain. Here we approach it from a text which has never before been made the centre-piece of a book-length study, the *Life of St Germanus, bishop of Auxerre* by Constantius of Lyon. A fifth-century text about a fifth-century subject, and (what's more) one which has occasion to refer to events in Britain, is not to be lightly set aside. It is perhaps all the more remarkable, then, that since the controversies of the early twentieth century so little close attention has been devoted to Constantius's book. No doubt there is more of importance to be discovered about the history of the text. But Professor Thompson has taken Wilhelm Levison's edition as a basis for discussion and has launched into a thorough examination of Constantius's evidence for the history of the fifth-century West, and of Britain in particular.

The results are fascinating. Professor Thompson has brought his accumulated experience of forty years' reading and analysis of late Latin historical sources to bear on Constantius's efforts. Sometimes the reader will wince as Constantius's faults are exhibited for public display. But no one will come away from this book without a fundamentally better grasp of this important text and of the place of its evidence in the historian's reconstruction of fifth-century life. The qualities which have made Professor Thompson one of the leading – and controversial – exponents of the history of late Roman and sub-Roman Europe are all displayed here to the full. His studies of the Huns, of the Goths in their various manifestations, of the other Germanic peoples who penetrated the late Empire, and of the host-provinces have become classics. For some years now it has been becoming apparent that he has saved up for his retirement an assault on the literary sources for the history of fifth-century Britain. While occasional publications on this subject stretch back into the 1950s, since 1977 a steady flow of his papers has challenged assumptions and interpretations dear to students of British history. With a fresh eye, a Continental comparative perspective, and a closeness to text which others could well imitate, he has given a new impetus to historical study of the period.

It is difficult to know whether ancient or modern authors have been exposed to greater stress by this onset. Certainly, students of the period have been greatly challenged. And that process is carried remorselessly forward in this book. An assessment is achieved, tentatively at times but presented always in a lively and amusing style, of Constantius's *Life of St Germanus* and especially of its evidence for the history of Armorica and Britain. We are enabled to see Constantius's strengths and weaknesses, to discover something of his sources and methods. And there is clear gain here for our understanding of fifth-century Britain. Yet while this study proceeds from a close reading and analysis of the key-text, nonetheless Professor Thompson also allows such a consideration to form the basis for wide-ranging discussion of critical issues. The proponents of 'continuity' between (sub-)Roman and Anglo-Saxon in fifth-century Britain will find their most basic assumptions under ferocious attack. Those who have developed extended theories of the history of Anglo-Saxon kingship must now contend with Professor Thompson's insistence that the evidence is against the Saxons' living under kingly rule at the time of their settlement in Britain.

That the Britons of southern and eastern England were for the most part slaughtered or driven from their homes in a period beginning in the mid-fifth century is an old and very unfashionable idea which begins to live strongly again as a result of Professor Thompson's ministrations. It is not the only aspect of his book which will provoke a reaction. He does not claim to have said the last word about Constantius's evidence and indeed it is clear that there are other aspects of the *Life of St Germanus* which will repay study. Professor Thompson has stressed heavily a particular aspect of Constantius's hagiography; the author's intentions in the work as a whole, and in particular sections, remain a question for further research. In volume 5 of this series, which Professor Thompson had not seen when he wrote his book, it was questioned whether Constantius's 'Hallelujah victory' was even to be taken at face-value. The extent of the rhetorical, literary element in Constantius's writing remains to be determined. And some may think that Professor Thompson's discussion of Constantius's account of St Germanus's second visit to Britain could be held to provide a detailed underpinning of Nora Chadwick's theory that it was a mere doublet of the narrative of the visit of 429, a hypothesis which has perhaps never received from students the detailed consideration which it deserves. That would not be Professor Thompson's view: indeed he locks the account of the second visit into a compelling argument that the death of St Germanus in Italy occurred as early as A.D. 437.

For the student of the late Roman and early mediaeval world, this book offers much original food for thought. Among old favourites like the Bacaudae, one will find new objects of Thompsonian criticism like the British Pelagians. One can only wonder where the author will strike next. In the meantime, the general editor would like to record his pleasure at being able to act as host to this particularly fascinating contribution to an irresistibly attractive field of study.

David Dumville
Girton College, Cambridge
September 1983

Preface

It is strange that students of Roman Britain have paid so little attention to Constantius's *Life of St Germanus of Auxerre*. We cannot afford to ignore any ancient author who speaks at some length about Britain, and yet British scholars have rarely lingered over Constantius's *Life*. It can hardly be that they think this limpid narrative to call for no criticism, for the narrative is anything but limpid. On the contrary, the monstrous difficulties of interpreting works of hagiography may well have discouraged even the stoutest hearts among students of fifth-century Britain. For my part, I have more than once almost given up in despair, feeling myself driven from time to time to conclude that Constantius's chapters on Britain are worthless, that we cannot even be wholly sure (to cite one example only) that Germanus visited the island twice, and that Nora Chadwick may have been right when she suggested that the second visit is a mere doublet of the first. And yet, here and there in the British narrative, there are assertions which cannot easily be written off as mere inventions – the man of tribunician power, for instance, and the unparalleled combination of Picts and Saxons who failed to fight at Easter 429 (though in communicating with one another they overcame a mountainous language-barrier), and the latinised Greek name of Elafius, the only fifth-century Briton whom Constantius mentions by name.

In my opinion, then, it is difficult to resist the twin conclusion that Constantius knew certain facts about the visit or visits of Germanus to Britain and that his account cannot be wholly written off as worthless. But how much he knew and to what extent we can trust his words are questions of the darkest obscurity. I have stated my general conclusions on the value of the *Life* in the 'Introduction' to this book, but it would be folly to claim that other judgments may not be equally, or almost equally, tenable. And so throughout the book: the nature of the evidence is such that I have repeatedly set out conclusions though feeling that they may be to some extent subjective and that other students of Constantius might with much justice reach other conclusions. But that is the common fate of those who study the Lives of the saints; and perhaps my book will induce others to set out other and better conclusions on the religion, politics, historical geography, and so on, of Britain in the dismal years when, in the words of Constantius, 'the magnificent Aetius was governing the republic'.

My warm thanks are due to Professor Robert Markus (Nottingham) and to the general editor of the series. I blush to think of the number and the size of the mistakes from which they saved me. But they are in no way to blame for the mistakes which remain, or for the conclusions reached, or for the heretical opinions which I have championed.

E. A. Thompson
July 1983

I

INTRODUCTION

Constantius of Lyon wrote the *Life* of Saint Germanus, bishop of Auxerre, probably in the decade 480–90, at any rate before 494. The little book contains no dates, but by good luck we can fix one event in the bishop's life without doubt: his first visit to Britain is dated in Prosper's *Chronicle* to the year 429. Constantius's account of the saint's life before that event is sketchy, but by no means without interest. On the other hand, the description of Germanus's life after his return from Britain is of the utmost value. It gives us a vivid description of a bishop's life in Gaul in the second quarter of the fifth century, a description which abounds in place-names, personal names, titles of rank and office, and so on. At an unknown date Germanus returned to Britain for a short while, but of this second visit Constantius could evidently discover very little. With the saint's second return to Auxerre the vivacious and detailed narrative resumes. Germanus became involved in a great revolt of Armorica. True, the narrative does not take us into the interior of Armorica and we see nothing of life in the rebellious northwest of Gaul. We see the rebels only from the outside. We see them only in the impact which they made on the Western authorities. Germanus then travelled to the Imperial court at Ravenna so as to obtain an amnesty for the rebels, and the description of this journey from Auxerre to Ravenna is extraordinarily informative. At Ravenna Germanus met members of the Imperial family, including the Emperor Valentinian III himself, and in that city he died. The *Life* ends with a description of the return of the saint's body to his native Auxerre. The *Life* of Germanus by Constantius together with the *Life* of Severinus by Eugippius are among the most vivid, lively, and instructive texts to have survived from the Western Roman Empire in the fifth century.[1]

Thanks to Constantius, then, the last events in the history of sub-Roman Britain of which we have relatively detailed knowledge are the two visits paid to that island by Germanus, bishop of Auxerre. Besides Constantius's *Life*,

[1] On the date of the *Vita* see Levison, 'Bischof Germanus', p. 112; Bardy, 'Constance', pp. 96–7. For an account in English of this Constantius see Chadwick, *Poetry and Letters*, pp. 285–8. On the question of how the hagiographers used their sources see Delehaye, *Les légendes*, p. 57, although Constantius must, of course, be classed with Eugippius and Sulpicius Severus as one of those who belong to the highest class of hagiographer and to whom, therefore, Delehaye's considerations do not fully apply.

1

the *Chronicle* and the *Contra Collatorem* of Prosper of Aquitaine give us some further information about the first of the two visits which Germanus paid to Britain. It is well for us that the *Chronicle* of Prosper gives us the date 429 for the first visit for, if we had to rely on Constantius alone, we should hardly be able to date it even to the nearest decade. We could know only that it must have taken place before 439, the latest year in which Auxiliaris can have been Praetorian Prefect of Gaul,[2] for this visit to Britain took place before Germanus went to Arles to see Auxiliaris when he was still Prefect, but how long before 439 no one could tell, were it not for Prosper. As far as I know, Prosper's date has never been questioned. Germanus visited the island for the second time (it is usually thought) in the 440s; but I shall argue that 437 is perhaps a more likely year.[3]

No one knows how a fifth-century hagiographer began to write his work, but we may be sure that he did not start by rushing to consult the nearest copy of a chronicle. That is to say, he did not begin by mapping out the chronology of his hero's life or even by fixing the dates of his birth and death. As we have seen, there are no dates at all in the *Life* of Germanus. Few problems were of less importance in the hagiographer's eyes than problems of chronology. The hagiographer's aim was to glorify his hero and to edify his reader: he had no ambition to write history. Hagiography was one thing, history most decidedly another. Accordingly, when Eugippius speaks of the death of St Severinus in what is now Austria, he remarks that it took place on 8 January. It does not occur to him to say in what year the holy man expired. The saint's day was important: the year of his death was not. For Constantius it was worth while recording that the battle against the Picts and Saxons took place at Easter, for that fact was relevant to his story. But Easter of which year? That was a question which was not worth raising: it was beside the point, and I am sure that it never occurred to Constantius to record it and that it never occurred to his readers to expect him to do so. It follows that Constantius had no reason to ask himself whether Germanus visited Britain in 429 or in 430 or in 431, and so on. Nor did it appear to be relevant to his work of edification to say that the year in which the second visit took place was 437 or 447 or some other year. As far as he was concerned, the exact year was of no consequence whatever. Germanus's works would not appear more edifying if they were known to have been performed in 429 than if they were known to have been performed in 430. In fact, Constantius held the not unreasonable belief that there is only a limited amount of spiritual uplift to be gained from the study of chronology. And with this opinion (if they had ever formulated it) his readers would have been in wholehearted agreement. They had opened his book in search of inspiration, and to learn that Germanus probably visited Britain in 437 rather than in 447 would be somewhat less than inspiring.

Indeed, writing some forty or fifty years after the event, Constantius might

[2] See p. 67 below.
[3] See pp. 55–70 below.

2

not have found it at all easy to discover the date of the second visit, supposing that he had set himself to find out. Prosper, who was a chronicler writing only four years after the first visit, very properly recorded its date; but, when he continued his *Chronicle* several years later, he did not think the second visit worth mentioning or did not know that it had happened. By his own standards he had done full justice to Germanus in his entry under the year 429, and there was no need to repeat the tribute. It might have been exceedingly difficult, perhaps impossible, for Constantius to discover even approximately in what year Germanus had crossed the Ocean for the second time. Beyond a doubt Constantius would have considered it labour lost to travel about in search of someone who could establish the exact year. And the passage of Eugippius in which he omits to tell us the year of his hero's death shows that the fact of Germanus's dying in the very year of the second visit to Britain did not make it likely that the year would be identified or identifiable. Germanus died on 31 July.[4] That was known. That was important. Constantius probably never asked himself, nor did his readers expect him to ask himself, in what year 31 July saw the death of the holy man of Auxerre. Indeed, it is far from certain that Constantius could have said in what year the first visit to Britain had taken place. It is not clear that Lupus himself, who had accompanied Germanus in 429, was able in the last few years before he died (perhaps in 478/9) to remember the precise year. Could he have named the consuls of that year? Could Constantius have named them?

It may be objected to some of the arguments put forward in the following pages that they involve taking Constantius's words too literally. Some of my arguments actually turn on the interpretation of a single word, such as *reliquerat*[5] and even *uel*.[6] Perhaps the criticism is justified: but we can argue only on the basis of such evidence as exists, and these arguments are based on what Constantius tells us, not on what we think that he ought to have told us or on what he might have said if he had chosen to write at greater length or in a different style or in another genre.

On the other hand, we are not justified in arguing that Constantius, writing fifty or sixty years after 429, can have known only the broad outline of events which had happened in Britain so long ago and that the details must be flourishes of his own invention designed to glorify Germanus. That may sometimes be the case, but scepticism can be carried too far. For British affairs, for example, Lupus, bishop of Troyes – who accompanied Germanus on the first visit to Britain –, lived to an advanced age (dying, it seems, only in 478/9), and so he could have been available to supply information to Constantius: this is a matter to which we shall return.[7] Of course, we must not expect that Constantius would examine Lupus or any other witness and

---

[4] On this date see p. 57, n. 10, below.
[5] See p. 47 below.
[6] See p. 73f. below.
[7] See p. 82 below.

cross-examine him, and check and cross-check him, as we might expect a modern enquirer to do: Constantius, as I have said, was not aiming at writing history. On the other hand, we cannot write off the explicit statements of the *Life* as though they were arbitrary inventions of the author. We might guess with some confidence that he did indeed meet with exceptional difficulties in collecting information about the second British visit, for his narrative of the second visit is woefully inadequate.[8] But he did not fill in the gaps in his information with tales of his own invention, or at any rate he did not often do so, and recent writers have not followed Nora Chadwick when she remarks of the second visit that 'nothing is related as happening, nothing is effected', and goes on to doubt whether the second visit ever took place: might it not be a mere doublet of the first visit? That is in my wavering opinion to go too far. What would Constantius or any of his informants have gained by inventing such a fiction, especially when, as Mrs Chadwick remarks, little is related as happening? Hanson perhaps puts it more correctly: 'it may be doubted if Constantius knew anything about this second visit, except that it took place'.[9] But, oddly enough, it is in his account of the second visit that Constantius gives us his one and only British proper name (apart from St Alban). This is the personal name Elafius, and there is no reason whatever for thinking that this is Constantius's own invention. The incident in which the name occurs could have been an invention of the author, but how would it reflect glory on Germanus to say that the name of the lame boy's father was Elafius? I think that, when Germanus paid his second visit to Britain, he came in contact with a man named Elafius, although the circumstances of the meeting may be far from clear. On this second visit the saint was accompanied by a bishop called Severus; of him we know nothing beyond what Constantius tells us, and that is very little. When Constantius was collecting information for the *Life* Severus was apparently dead or otherwise unavailable. We have no reason to think that he survived until that time and that Constantius could have questioned him.[10] Otherwise, Constantius could hardly have known so little.

A major difficulty is caused to the modern student by the problem of arguments from Constantius's silence on various matters. Here are one or two examples. Germanus voyaged across the English Channel on four occasions. In Constantius's description of these four voyages there is no reference to Saxon pirates and no hint that they might have formed a threat to the traveller or that the bishop was lucky to have escaped them or that he or Constantius ever even gave them a thought. But is it legitimate to infer from this silence that Saxon pirates were unknown, or even that they were rarely seen, in the Channel at this date? In the year 429 itself one party of Saxons may indeed have crossed from the Continent to Britain, the party

---

[8] See p. 84 below.

[9] Hanson, *Saint Patrick*, p. 50; Chadwick, *Poetry and Letters*, p. 259.

[10] Bede, *Historia Ecclesiastica*, I.21, makes Severus bishop of Trier. Like everything which Bede writes, this must be treated with respect; but it is not easy to see how authentic information on the point could have reached him.

which Germanus helped to defeat at Easter in that year (if these Saxons were indeed invaders rather than men who had already settled in Britain). If so, these Saxons were on the high seas as early as March or April.[11] Did the rest of the summer witness no other band of raiders? No one knows the answer to that question. It is not impossible, for example, that at this date, although Saxon ships may have crossed often enough from the Continent to Britain, they normally did so to the east of the route taken by Germanus. In this case, it seems, an argument from silence in either direction could scarcely be justified.

We have asserted that the purpose of Constantius's *Life* is the glorification of Germanus and the edification of his readers. But there are certain claims which Constantius does not put forward. For example, he does not say explicitly that the saint was able in the end to convert the leaders of the British Pelagians to Catholicism in 429. Look at *Vita*, § 14.[12] His silence in that passage seems to outweigh his later vague generalisation in which he tells us that the heresy disappeared 'from the minds of mankind'.[13] But if that had been the case, the saint's second visit would have been a work of supererogation. In this matter, then, the argument from silence may well be legitimate: the leading Pelagians did not go over to orthodoxy. Again, the old charge that Constantius ought to have mentioned St Patrick and his stay at Auxerre and his instruction by St Germanus must also be abandoned, for most experts seem now to agree that Patrick probably never set foot in Gaul, to say nothing of Auxerre, much though he would have liked to do so.[14] In fact, Constantius probably never heard of Patrick. Patrick was buried in a mysterious silence for the century and a half which followed on his death.[15] Bede was interested in the Church in Ireland and reports what he could learn of it – for example, the mission of Palladius in 431.[16] But he does not mention Patrick, and I infer that he too had never heard of that extraordinary man. The right conclusion would appear to be that when Constantius omits to seize what we might think to be an obvious chance to glorify his hero he is in fact *either* concealing a setback or even a failure on Germanus's part *or else* he did not know of the matter in question.[17]

In general, no rule can be laid down about this matter of inferences from Constantius's silence. Each case ought to be judged irrespective of the others. On the whole, it must be concluded that in some instances Constantius's silence may be instructive but that the interpretation of each case calls for tact and restraint.

Finally, I return to what is beyond doubt the most intractable problem

[11] See pp. 39–46 below.
[12] *Vita*, 261, 20–2.
[13] § 15 (262,9).
[14] Patrick, *Confessio*, § 43. See Binchy, 'Patrick', pp. 80–90, and Hanson, *Saint Patrick*, p. 129f. But contrast Thomas, *Christianity*, pp. 321–7.
[15] Binchy, 'Patrick', pp. 168–71.
[16] *Historia Ecclesiastica*, I.13; V.24.
[17] See, for example, p. 27 below.

which we encounter when we try to estimate Constantius's contribution to the history of Britain: how far can we press the literal meaning of his words? For example, he mentions a Briton 'of tribunician power'. Why should he have invented this term if he had merely wished to show his hero in the company of an important Briton? Why not describe the stranger as a 'king' or a 'tyrant' or a 'magistrate' or a 'rich man' or by some such simple term as would immediately impress his readers? Constantius seems to be making an attempt to be precise: he seems to wish his readers to understand that, although the man was not what his readers in Gaul would take to be a tribune, yet he was something of that kind, something like a tribune. The implication appears to be that Constantius knew the nature of the man's authority and is trying to explain it. He is giving the nearest Roman equivalent of the man's office. Although even that deduction is somewhat subjective, yet my own opinion here is that Constantius had *some* detailed and accurate information about this incident of the first British visit.

But can we therefore go on to infer that Constantius is also correct in implying that the man of tribunician power took no part in the debate on Pelagianism, that he came forward out of the crowd only when the debate was over, and that there is no reason whatever for regarding him as a government-official whose task was to keep an eye on the proceedings? In fact, I have accepted all these three inferences.[18] But is that justified? I can reply only that this is what Constantius appears to have thought. If we may judge by his words, we must conclude that, when he visualised the incident of the man of tribunician power, he saw him as not playing any sectarian or political role. If then we assert that he played either or both of these parts, we are going beyond the evidence: we are reading things into the evidence which are not there. Although we have information from no other source, we are claiming to know more about the incident than Constantius knew.

There are two matters on which we have a second source of information in addition to Constantius's narrative. Prosper of Aquitaine tells us in his *Chronicle* of the circumstances in which Germanus was sent to Britain in 429, and the same author in his *Contra Collatorem* tells us something about the exiling of British Pelagians. In both cases it is hardly open to doubt that the version of events given by Prosper is preferable to that of Constantius, and that the narrative of Constantius is open to grave doubt. Yet to reject what Constantius wrote – apart from these two incidents and apart from matters where his version of events is self-evidently absurd – would be tantamount to holding that the *Life* is worthless as a source of historical information. After much wavering I find that conclusion difficult to accept. To reject all the statements of ancient historians (to say nothing of hagiographers) where they cannot be supported by external evidence would be to reject huge areas of what we call ancient history. Indeed, would not such an attitude entail rejecting those two passages of Prosper of Aquitaine where they are contradicted by Constantius?

[18] See p. 26f. below.

6

II

CONSTANTIUS ON BRITAIN, GAUL, AND ITALY

There is a mysterious, uncharacteristic vagueness in the language which Constantius uses when he speaks of Britain and its inhabitants. This vagueness, this cloudiness is in sharp contrast to the precise language of those of his pages which tell of Germanus's activities in Gaul and Italy. There arrived in Gaul, he says, a 'legation' from Britain. The legation announced that in their country – *in locis suis*, 'in their country', 'over there', 'in Britain' – Pelagianism had won successes and that help ought to be sent to the Catholic faith there.[1] Who sent this deputation, *legatio*? Of whom was it composed – clerics or laymen? From which part of Britain did it come? Why does Constantius use as vague a phrase as 'over there', *in locis suis*? Why does he not tell us exactly where the danger threatened? And who were the Pelagians of Britain? Who was their leader? What was the nature of the crisis which caused the Catholics to call for help as a matter of urgency (*quam primum*)?[2] Constantius gives no answer to any one of these or similar questions. That is not at all his manner when he is speaking about Gaul and Italy, as we shall see. And yet we might have expected that some knowledge of these matters would have survived at Auxerre or Lyon.

At any rate, the legation was evidently sent not by random Britons but by some sort of British organisation, for when Germanus arrived in Britain a meeting with the Pelagians had been arranged for him. There is no hint that a mere scratch-meeting had been scraped together at the last minute when his arrival in Britain was imminent. Some kind of British organisation had taken the decision to send a delegation, had appointed its members, received the Gallic bishops' reply, and arranged a meeting with the Pelagians at which the heresy could be, and was, debated. But of the organisation which achieved all this Constantius says not a syllable. Whether this organisation extended over a large or only a small area of Britain is wholly unknown. When the delegation said that a crisis had arisen *in locis suis* we do not know whether they had a specific area in mind. The words in fact mean nothing more precise than 'in those parts', just as Hugh Williams rendered them.[3] So

---

[1] *Vita*, § 12 (259,6). All references are to the chapters, pages, and lines of Levison's edition: Krusch & Levison, *Passiones*, VII.247–83.
[2] *Ibid*. (259,7).
[3] Williams, *Christianity*, p. 224.

we cannot even guess at the nature of the organisation which set these events in motion. There is certainly no reason to think that anything as formal as a synod had assembled in Britain in order to organise the delegation and formulate the appeal to the Catholics on the Continent. Happily, we have a second account of the circumstances in which Germanus paid his first visit to Britain, the account of Prosper of Aquitaine; and we shall see that this gives a different description of what happened.[4] But before we compare the two accounts of the preliminaries to the first British visit, let us look at what Constantius tells us about Britain itself and conditions there.

For some reason Constantius usually refers to the people of Britain as *populus*[5] or *populi*.[6] Only once does he call the people *plebem*, and even there we find *populum* as a variant reading.[7] But during the narrative of Germanus's activities in Gaul the word *plebs* is often the term for the Gallic populace. In §§ 7–8 of the *Life* the term *plebs* occurs four times in reference to the Gauls,[8] and in addition Constantius speaks of *plebs urbana uel rustica*,[9] *prouincialibus*,[10] and *ciues*,[11] but *populus, populi* elsewhere.[12] I do not know what is the significance of the fact that he practically always calls the people *populus* in Britain but more often than not *plebs* in Gaul, although the instances in each case seem to be numerous enough to suggest that he had some purpose in mind in making this distinction.[13] And the matter is not made any simpler by the fact that in his chapters on Germanus's activities in Italy – or, more precisely, in the three cities of Milan, Ravenna,[14] and Piacenza (Placentia) – Constantius speaks of the inhabitants as *populus*[15] or more frequently as *populi*.[16] He never uses the word *plebs* in connexion with Italians.

When narrating events in Gaul and Italy he uses a dozen place- and river-names. For example, he names five Gallic cities (Auxerre, Autun, Alesia, Arles, and Lyon) and four Italian cities (Rome, Ravenna, Milan, Piacenza). In referring to Britain he names none. On the Continent he speaks of an *oppidum*,[17] of *urbs*,[18] of *prouinciae*,[19] and often of *ciuitas*.[20] In one

---

[4] For a comparison of Constantius's account with that of Prosper, see pp. 79–81 below.
[5] *Vita*, §14 (261,10, 13, 22; 262,4, 9); §17 (264,10).
[6] *Ibid.*, §12 (259,6); §27 (270,17).
[7] *Ibid.* (270,18).
[8] On pp. 255–6 of Levison's text: Krusch & Levison, *Passiones*, VII.
[9] *Vita*, §2 (252,2).
[10] *Ibid.*, §7 (254,10).
[11] *Ibid.*, §19 (265,17); §24 (269,13).
[12] *Ibid.*, §6 (254,5); §7 (255,12); §8 (256,9); §23 (268,1).
[13] His usage is puzzling. At §6 (254,5) *populi* refers to the countrypeople outside Auxerre, but at §7 (255,12) it means the inhabitants of Auxerre who are called *plebs* twice in the next two lines. At §8 (256,9) *populus* means the people of (presumably) Auxerre, who are *plebs* in the next line.
[14] Ravenna is described as *ciuitas* at §47 (281,4).
[15] *Vita*, §32 (274,17); §32 (275,4).
[16] *Ibid.*, §35 (276,8); §36 (277,15); §37 (277,21); §38 (279,8); §45 (282,11).
[17] *Ibid.*, §1 (251,1); §6 (254,3).
[18] *Ibid.*, §7 (255,2); §23 (267,20; 268,7); §33 (275,6) on Milan.
[19] *Ibid.*, §1 (251,11).
[20] *Ibid.*, §7 (254,14); §19 (265,14, 19); §20 (266,1); §23 (268,4, 9); §24 (269,12); §31 (274,6).

passage he even mentions the *territorium ciuitatis suae*,[21] in another *territorium Augustudunense*,[22] and elsewhere *uici omnes, municipia, ciuitates*.[23] When he talks of Britain, on the other hand, Constantius never uses the words *ciuitas*, *oppidum*, *urbs*, *municipium*, or *territorium*. Nor are the inhabitants ever *ciues* or *prouinciales*. When he says that the visiting bishops preached *non solum in ecclesiis, uerum etiam per triuia, per rura, per deuia*,[24] he certainly does not imply the existence of cities (although this has often been inferred). He means simply that they preached in churches (without any indication of where these churches were sited) and at cross-roads and in the open air in the country-side, even in out-of-the-way parts of the countryside. Instead of the Roman terms for administrative areas (province, *ciuitas*, and so on), Constantius when he is referring to Britain speaks vaguely of the 'region'. The preachers win over the *regionis uniuersitas*.[25] They leave Britain *cum totius maerore regionis*.[26] Elafius – this rather than 'Elafus' is the correct form of this latinised Greek name[27] – is the chief man *regionis illius*;[28] and when Constantius adds *hunc Elafium prouincia tota subsequitur*,[29] few will think that one of the old Roman provinces of Britain still survived and that its inhabitants now flocked to follow Elafius. The phrase simply means that the whole 'area' or 'neigh-bourhood' followed him, and indeed it is used as a synonym of *regio*, the region of which Elafius was the leading man.[30] The Pelagian ringleaders were banished *ut et regio absolutione et illi emendatione fruerentur*.[31] The result in Britain, according to Constantius, is that the faith lasts to this day un-impaired *in illis locis*,[32] a phrase of which we have already seen the almost meaningless meaning.

The obvious explanation of some of these facts is no doubt that the old Roman administrative units – the provinces and the *ciuitates* with their *territoria* – had disappeared by 429 in the 'region' which Germanus visited, whereas, of course, they had by no means disappeared from Gaul; and Constantius does not mention *ciues* or *prouinciales* in Britain because he knew that the inhabitants were Roman citizens or provincials no longer.

Certainly, as I mentioned above, it is a mistake to appeal to the *Life* for proof that city-life still continued in Britain in 429. There is no explicit

[21] *Ibid.*, §20 (266.1).
[22] *Ibid.*, §30 (273.14).
[23] *Ibid.*, §21 (267.1). Observe that Auxerre is *oppidum*, §6 (254.3), *ciuitas*, §7 (254.14), *urbs*, §6 (255.2), all in the space of a few lines.
[24] *Ibid.*, §14 (261.2).
[25] *Ibid.* (261.6).
[26] *Ibid.*, §18 (265.9).
[27] Levison, 'Bischof Germanus', p. 126, n. 1. For another 'Aelafius' see Jones *et al.*, *The Prosopography*, I.16.
[28] *Vita*, §26 (270.2); but see p. 12 below.
[29] *Ibid.*, §26 (270.6).
[30] Grosjean, 'Notes', p. 177, n. 1, shows restraint when he writes, 'il n'est pas assuré . . . que Constance donne à *provincia* sa valeur exacte et technique'.
[31] *Vita*, §27 (270.20). Contrast §40 (280.1) *Armoricanae regionis* (cf. §28 [271.5]), where the place-name makes all the difference. Armorica is (correctly) a number of *prouinciae* at §28 (272.17); and a *regio* at §40 (280.1).
[32] §27 (271.2). See p. 85 below.

mention of cities anywhere in the chapters which deal with Britain. There is not the slightest suggestion that they still survived. What the silence of the *Life* suggests, if anything, is that city-life had disappeared in the area of Britain of which Constantius is speaking. And yet in recent years archaeologists have begun to tell us with increasing confidence that life did indeed continue in the British cities, or some of them, well into the fifth century, perhaps as late as 450 in some cases, or even later.[33] But whether there was any administrative organisation in them such as Constantine the Great, say, or even Magnus Maximus would have recognised is unknown. Certainly, nothing of the kind is recorded by Constantius: for him Britain is a land without cities or *ciuitates* or *curiales* ('city-councillors'). At first sight there is in this matter a contradiction between what Constantius tells us and what the archaeological evidence shows to have been the case.

On the other hand, in his pages Gaul and Italy are places where not only the cities but even the familiar Roman offices still survive. We are told that Germanus *tribunalia praefecturae professione aduocationis ornauit;*[34] that is to say, he had practised as an advocate in the court of the Urban or Praetorian Prefect.[35] We hear of the *ducatus culmen et regimen per prouincias*[36] and of the *apicem praefecturae.*[37] We read of the time *cum princeps praesidalis militauit* [sc. *Ianuarius*] *officii,*[38] and this Ianuarius was taking *solidi* to the provincial governor at Sens (*ciuitas Senonum*), for Sens, not Auxerre, was the provincial capital of the province of Lugdunensis Senonia. The *tributaria functio* still exists,[39] and *euectiones*, 'travel-warrants', are still issued to travellers using the public post in Gaul[40] as well as in Italy.[41] Communications in Gaul are still open and easy. Horse-thieves, and other thieves, seem to be no more frequently met with than they had ever been. Ianuarius was, as we have seen, an important official under the provincial governor and apparently felt himself able to travel to his headquarters, carrying the *solidi* which had been raised in taxes, without being accompanied by any bodyguard or protection of any kind.[42] He was not directly set upon and robbed, but when he rather unwisely dropped the sack in which he was carrying the *solidi*, the man who chanced to find it was somewhat less than honest. He could have pleaded that Ianuarius's carelessness in losing the bag had led him into temptation. Clearly, he was not a professional brigand. In Constantius's pages there is

---

[33] See the discussion with references in Todd, *Roman Britain*, pp. 241–2, and Wacher, *The Towns*, pp. 220–3, 238, 276f., 312–15, 389.

[34] *Vita*, § 1 (251,8).

[35] Jones *et al.*, *The Prosopography*, II.504.

[36] *Vita*, § 1 (251,11). See p. 84f. below.

[37] *Vita*, § 37 (268,13).

[38] *Ibid.*, § 7 (254,10).

[39] *Ibid.*, § 19 (265,16).

[40] *Ibid.* (265,21); § 20 (266,7).

[41] *Ibid.*, § 44 (282,3). Notice the rare use of *euectio* at § 19 (265,21) and § 20 (266,8) to mean 'horse'. The *Thesaurus Linguae Latinae*, V.1006,40, quotes only the Theodosian Code, VIII.5,41, as a parallel.

[42] *Vita*, § 7 (254,10).

still apparently a distinction between *maiores personae* and *mediocres personae*.[43] Leporius is called by the technical term *uir spectabilis*.[44] And Constantius mentions more than one of the old offices as still existing in Italy.[45] As his latest editor says of him, 'To read him you would not imagine that his hero lived, and that he himself was still living, in that terrible fifth century which saw the disappearance of the Western Roman Empire'.[46]

It is Constantius's normal, though not invariable, practice to tell us the name of each individual of whom he speaks and to say something of his post or his rank (as Leporius is called *uir spectabilis*). True, he does not do so in the case of some of the humbler people who are helped miraculously by the saint[47] or in the case of the various villains of his narrative.[48] But in general he is exceedingly exact and explicit, far more so than Sulpicius Severus in his *Vita Sancti Martini*. In fact, Constantius is meticulous and precise, by the standards of writers of his time, in recording not only names[49] but also official titles of persons on the Continent.

When he comes to speak of Britain his procedure is very different. The one or two official titles (if we may call them that) which he reports from Britain are notoriously imprecise, and out of character with his work elsewhere, as well as alien to the Imperial administrative system. One man is described as *uir tribuniciae potestatis*.[50] This man, when he took on his title or when he was given it by a superior, may have had in mind the powers of a military tribune (although it is merely a coincidence that late in the sixth century in Italy the tribune in command of the local garrison became governor of the local city, a state of affairs which is not known to have been the case in the fifth century).[51] But indeed it is by no means certain that the title was a military one at all rather than an administrative one. Or perhaps tribunician power was merely a vague high-sounding title, redolent of the old days of Imperial rule, which would impress the local people very much as 'field-marshal' and 'emperor' and even 'messiah' have been used by more recent potentates in Africa. Certainly, there is no compelling reason for thinking that the man of tribunician power was the chief 'magistrate' or ruler of his district; Hugh Williams (who produced that heroic translation of Gildas in 1899–1901) goes too far in calling him 'a kind of prince'.[52] For all we know, he may have been a subordinate officer in an army commanded by someone else or an admin-

---

[43] *Ibid.*, § 11 (258,21); § 22 (267,8).

[44] *Ibid.*, § 33 (275,13).

[45] *Ibid.*, § 38 (278,1); § 39 (279,10).

[46] Borius, *Constance*, p. 24. But travel in Gaul was not always easy: see Sidonius, *Epistulae*, IX.3,1f., referring perhaps to A.D. 475/6.

[47] *Vita*, § 11 (258,21), *mediocrium personarum successit hospitio* (they are unnamed); § 29 (272,21f.); § 30 (273,16); § 45 (282,7).

[48] *Ibid.*, § 7 (254,13); § 20 (266,3); § 32 (274,17).

[49] On this quality of his, see Bardy, 'Constance', p. 107, although Bardy is clearly using the later, interpolated, text of the *Vita*.

[50] *Vita*, § 15 (261,23).

[51] Jones, *The Later Roman Empire*, I.313; II.760.

[52] Williams, *Christianity*, p. 225.

istrator working under the direction of a superior administrator. He seems to have had a local importance of some sort, but Constantius says nothing whatever which would suggest that the man of tribunician power was one of the 'tyrants' who, according to Procopius, ruled Britain after 410.

Another man appears to be described (§ 26) as *regionis illius primus*,[53] which can hardly be an official title or even a paraphrase of an official title. The phrase is more probably a mere descriptive epithet, indicating that he was (or had the reputation of being) either the richest man of the neighbourhood or the most powerful 'strong man' or both. But perhaps it does not mean even that. Here is the sentence in which this person is introduced: 'Elafius quidam regionis illius primus in occursum sanctorum . . . properauit . . . hunc Elafium prouincia tota subsequitur.'[54] I have often wondered whether in this passage Constantius does not mean us to take the words *quidam regionis illius* together, and *primus* with *in occursum sanctorum . . . properauit*. Elafius, a man of that region, was the first person to hurry to meet the holy bishops, and then after him came the rest of the 'province'. True, to call Elafius *quidam regionis illius* would appear rather banal, but no more so than to describe, as Constantius does elsewhere, a woman of Piacenza as *matrona quaedam loci eius*.[55] Be that as it may, this man, unlike the man of tribunician power, could have been one of the 'usurpers', *tyranni*, who took over the government of Britain after Roman power had disappeared.[56] But in fact the term is probably one which Constantius made up for the occasion. Germanus was alleged to have cured someone's son, and the writer makes this person out to be a man of importance. In view of the extreme difficulty which Constantius encountered in trying to obtain information about the second visit to Britain,[57] it would be rash to suppose that he had precise knowledge of Elafius's position in life, and about that alone. He certainly has precise knowledge of nothing else connected with the second visit. At all events, such terms or titles take us into the sub-Roman world of the Moors, for example, where we find a 'king' and a 'prefect' and even an 'emperor', and so on.[58] As in the matter of the existence of the cities, the contrast between Gaul and Britain in Constantius's pages is sharp. It is not until long afterwards (in 486/7) that we find a *rex Romanorum* in Gaul.[59]

These differences between the passages of the *Vita* which tell of Germanus in Britain and those which speak of him in Gaul and Italy are so obvious that they cannot possibly be accidental. Such an accident – or rather, such a consistent series of accidents – would hardly be conceivable. They are certainly not a stylistic device, for they bring no stylistic gain. Nor can they

[53] *Vita*, § 26 (270,2).
[54] *Ibid.* (270,2f., 6).
[55] *Ibid.*, § 45 (282,7).
[56] Procopius, *Bellum Vandalicum*, III.2,38.
[57] See p. 84 below.
[58] Courtois, *Les Vandales*, pp. 333–9.
[59] Jones *et al.*, *The Prosopography*, II.1041. Cf. Arbogast, 'Count of Trier', *ca* 477: Sidonius, *Epistulae*, IV.17.

indicate a planned change of method on Constantius's part. Since he is so profuse with geographical information when dealing with Gaul and Italy, he can hardly have thought that his readers' interest in geography would instantly evaporate when he came to deal with Britain. Yet he must surely have known the names of the Channel ports and of London and of the other major cities of southern Britain, so that some sort of geographical description ought to have been within his powers. Even if he had been wholly ignorant of the conditions which Germanus had found across the Ocean, he would inevitably have used the terms current in the Roman world in which he lived, or at any rate an occasional such term would have slipped into his narrative through an oversight – some such word as *ciuitas* or *oppidum* or *territorium*. But in fact all such terms are rigorously excluded. There are no exceptional cases (unless we are to count *prouincia* in §26).[60] Were such terms excluded deliberately? But Constantius would hardly have wished to convey that there were no cities or towns in Britain, not merely in his own day, but also long ago at the time when Germanus had first visited the island in 429, for this would have thrown doubt on the value of Germanus's expedition: why worry about the condition of religion in a mere desert on the other side of the sea?

In my opinion, however, we are forced to the conclusion that the discrepancy between the British and the non-British parts of the narrative is in fact to be connected with the difficulty of collecting information about what had happened in Britain. Those events had taken place some fifty or sixty years before the date at which Constantius was writing. We know that he had difficulties in drawing up his narrative in general – not merely that part of it which concerns Britain – for he mentions them in his Preface and in his introductory letter to Patiens.[61] But the man who can tell us that forty or fifty years ago Volusianus held the post of *cancellarius* to the Master of the Soldiers, Sigisvult,[62] was a man who did not shrink from laborious historical research (even though he may have been guilty of a slip in this matter of Sigisvult).[63] It is inconceivable that his taste for research-work wilted when he came to deal with Britain or that he formed the conclusion that his readers would find Germanus's activities in Britain less uplifting than his activities on the mainland. The achievements of his saint were no less inspiring when they were performed in Britain than when they were performed on the Continent. The men who had accompanied Germanus to Britain in 429 and on his later visit will not have been numerous; and in the following fifty years or so death will have overtaken most of them, probably all of them. I find it hard to resist the conclusion – although this, too, is not without its difficulties – that Constantius gives us practically no details about Britain in the saint's time because he knew none. The trouble must have been that, while he had

---

[60] *Vita,* §26 (270,6).
[61] *Ibid.,* Praefatio (250,11; cf. 248,2).
[62] *Ibid.,* §38 (278,1).
[63] See p. 60f. below.

adequate sources of information about Gaul and Italy,[64] there was nobody who could tell him much about Britain. Indeed, we shall even see reason to think that he knew equally little about Britain as it had become in his own day.[65] It is sobering to notice that in the two passages of the *Vita* relating to Britain where we have a second source of information, Constantius's account of the events seems to be decidedly inferior. These are, first, the passage telling of the circumstances in which Germanus was sent to Britain in 429,[66] and, secondly, the passage relating how some of the saint's British Pelagian opponents were sent into exile.[67] In the latter Constantius's account is certainly less attractive than that of our second authority, and in the former it can hardly be doubted that Constantius's narrative is wholly conjectural and misleading. We must not be over-optimistic about our chances of learning much about the history of fifth-century Britain from his pages.

[64] But see p. 83 below.
[65] See p. 86 below.
[66] See p. 79 below.
[67] See p. 28 below.

III

RELIGION IN BRITAIN

Constantius leaves us in lamentable obscurity about the state of religion in Britain. But there is one question which he does answer. When Germanus preached *per triuia, per rura, per deuia*,[1] was he preaching to pagans in the countryside so as to convert them to christianity, or was he preaching so as to confirm the faith of the converted? Constantius leaves us in no doubt. The bishops preached (i) in order to strengthen the faith of the Catholics and (ii) so that those who had been misled by the Pelagian heretics might learn the path of correction.[2] That is to say, Germanus was doing what he had been sent to Britain to do: he was trying to retrieve the position of the Catholic Church in the relevant area of Britain. (It is interesting to find that the Church interfered for the first time outside the northern frontier of the Western Empire in order to pursue heretics. On the second such occasion – when it sent Palladius to Ireland in 431 to minister to the *Scotti* who believed in Christ – its purpose was less squalid: but even then it was *not* its avowed aim to convert the heathen.[3]) In 429 there was no question of trying to convert the heathen. The bishops had not been sent to Britain to act as missionaries for christianity in general and to win over pagans. They were there to fight heresy. Heresy was a more pressing problem than paganism. But to infer that Britain was mainly christian from the fact that the visitors did not try to convert the pagans would be wholly wrong. Moreover, Germanus and his companion spoke Latin. When they went out and preached *per triuia, per rura, per deuia*, on the first visit, they were not preaching to the peasants or the *coloni* or the rural slaves. These spoke British Celtic (which Germanus, we may take it, did not), and even if a relatively few of them had acquired some Latin, they would hardly have been able to follow an inspiring Latin sermon on the nature of Grace or a fiery Latin appeal to abandon the old

---

[1] § 14 (261,2).
[2] *Ibid.*
[3] Palladius incited the pope to send Germanus to Britain and was himself appointed as Ireland's first bishop. It is hard to resist the impression that the presence of the same man in both events implies some connexion between them. But we have not enough evidence to guess at what that connexion (if it existed) might have been.

15

gods and accept the doctrine of Original Sin![4] There is no reason to think that Germanus addressed the Celtic-speaking peasants through an interpreter: Constantius would probably have said so if that had been the case, for when in § 28 the saint spoke to the Alan King Goar Constantius says that he did so *medio interprete*.[5] In fact, there can hardly be any doubt that the poorer classes in the British countryside were still for the most part pagan. To take only one example or parallel from the Continent: in the first decade of the fifth century Maximus of Turin preached to the great landowners of his diocese in northern Italy. He makes it clear in his sermons over and over again that his congregation of landowners had only recently been converted from paganism to christianity: they were first-generation christians.[6] But the workers on their estates were still openly pagan, and the purpose of Maximus in some of his sermons is to urge the landowners to suppress this paganism.[7] It is improbable that the countryfolk of Britain, far away by the northern Ocean, even the countryfolk of southern Britain, had entered the Church as soon as those of the Turin region of Italy. And it is hardly possible to imagine circumstances in Britain changing radically in the next decade or so after Maximus had preached in Turin – changing, I mean, to the extent that the countrypeople of Britain were converted with dramatic speed. But we need not go as far afield as Italy for a parallel. When Germanus was appointed bishop, the people outside his own city of Auxerre were not yet christian: he founded his monastery within sight of the city on the other side of the river Yonne 'so that the people might be hurried to the Catholic faith', *ut ad fidem catholicam populi ... raperentur*,[8] (although in fact we never hear that he preached in person to these benighted pagans on his doorstep). There is abundant evidence to show that paganism and pagan practices and beliefs were exceedingly widespread among the peasantry of Gaul and Spain in the sixth century and beyond; and there is certainly no reason to think that the countrypeople of Britain were different in this respect at the time of Germanus's visits.

Constantius uses a phrase which may be significant in this connexion. Speaking of the baptism of the army which was soon to put to flight the Picts and Saxons at the Hallelujah battle, he says [*ecclesia*] *in expeditione campestri instar ciuitatis aptatur*.[9] The phrase has caused difficulty to translators. Hoare renders, 'on the plan of a city church, though set in a camp on active service'.

---

[4] On the languages of Britain see the fundamental statement of Jackson, *Language and History*, pp. 97–106, 255f., and the same scholar's fascinating summary in 'The British languages and their evolution'. In another paper, 'The British language', p. 61, Jackson states categorically that 'in the country the peasantry was entirely British-speaking'. Note also Rivet & Smith, *The Place-names*, pp. 10–29; and on the complexity of the situation see Thomas, *Christianity*, pp. 61–85.

[5] § 28 (272,7).

[6] See Maximus's *Sermo* LXIc, §4 (ed. Mutzenbecher, p. 258f.); *Sermo* LXIII, §2 (*ibid.*, p. 266f.); *Sermo* LXXIII, §3 (*ibid.*, p. 306,23); *Sermo* CVII (*ibid.*, p. 420).

[7] *Sermo* XCI, §2 (p. 369,23); *Sermo* CVII (p. 420).

[8] *Vita*, §6 (254.4).

[9] *Ibid.*, §17 (264.8).

It is true that *campestris* cannot have its Classical sense 'on the plain' as contrasted with 'among the hills'. It has its mediaeval sense of 'pertaining to the country' as distinct from the town, 'rural', in fact *champêtre*. The meaning is that 'a church was put together of interlaced branches, and although they were on an expedition in the countryside it was fitted out like a city[-church]'. There was no church, then, in the vicinity of the camp, and so the Britons constructed a rude one. But rude though it was, it was not what you would expect to find in the country. This one was like a city-church. (Observe that a city-baptistery, according to the archaeologists, might well be no more than a primitive wooden structure.[10]) On the other hand, Gildas makes it clear that churches and priests were commonplace in the cities in the fifth century; for when he comes to tell of the destruction of the British cities in the 460s and 470s he reports prominently the destruction of churches and clergy.[11] Indeed, Constantius's phrase *non solum in ecclesiis uerum etiam per triuia, per rura, per deuia*,[12] might well be taken to imply the absence of churches from the countryside and therefore their existence in cities: it is as near as he comes to mentioning cities.[13] The passage does not prove, however, that a country-church was an unknown phenomenon; but it does suggest that churches, even of this primitive type, were something which could not be said to be characteristic of the countryside. Beyond a doubt, the passage supports the view that the open countryside was still pagan in this part of Britain in 429; but the fact that Germanus preached *per triuia, per rura, per deuia* is evidence that christianity was not rigidly excluded from the countryside, although the phrase does not prove, of course, that christianity extended to the rural poor. There can be no doubt that the richer classes and the cities in southern Britain were in general christian. They had been so to a considerable extent even in the fourth century. If christianity, whether Catholic or Pelagian, was a mass-movement in early fifth-century Britain, it was an urban mass-movement, not a universal mass-movement.[14]

St Germanus's Latin-speaking congregations, then, both Catholic and Pelagian, were composed primarily of the townsfolk and of the relatively well-to-do, of persons who lived either in towns or in such villas as survived, whereas the poor countryfolk were heathen. (But I should not care to argue that this is why Constantius calls the British christians *populus* rather than *plebs*.[15]) When Germanus baptised the army which was to fight the invaders, had he converted them from paganism or from heresy or from neither? It is

[10] See Thomas, *Christianity*, pp. 214–27. He remarks (p. 218) that 'At Icklingham and Silchester . . . we can postulate timber baptistery sheds or buildings'. I take it that there is no need to argue the point that *ciuitatis* in the *Vita*, § 17 (264,9) does not imply the existence of a city in Britain.
[11] *De Excidio*, I.24.
[12] *Vita*, § 14 (261,2).
[13] See p. 9 above.
[14] For a wholly different view of the position of christianity in fifth-century Britain, see Hanson, *Saint Patrick*, pp. 34f., 69f., and the whole chapter: according to him, the Church claimed the loyalty 'probably of the majority of the population'.
[15] See p. 8 above.

not certain that christians – at all events, christians born of christian parents – were normally baptised as adults: infant-baptism was apparently normal. Jones remarks of late baptism that 'it is very difficult to estimate how common the practice was'.[16] He goes on to say that 'infant baptism was probably by now [the fifth century] normal for children of Christian parentage, though there were local variations of practice'. Unhappily, we have no information apart from the present passage about the custom in Britain. The matter is very obscure. Constantius says that the saint preached to these Britons daily. If he did so in Latin, they were presumably townsmen and villa-owners, and at this date we might expect such men to have been already christian. If the army was composed of pagan countryfolk, we should have expected to hear that Germanus preached through an interpreter. Which alternative is the more probable?

The evidence seems to incline slightly to support the view that these Britons were already christian and were now simply prepared for baptism and were in fact baptised by Germanus. The saint cannot have had more than two or three days, if so long, in which to instruct the men with his daily preachings (*cotidianis praedicationibus*),[17] for all the while the enemy was bearing down upon him and them. There was no time for an elaborate exposition of the christian faith, nor had the bishops been sent to Britain for the purpose of converting non-believers. Indeed, if they had converted the heathen on the eve of the battle, Constantius would hardly have missed the chance of pointing out the saint's all but superhuman achievement in winning over so many from the worship of the old gods in two or three days in circumstances of danger. But if they were already christian, though not baptised, it would have been nothing out of the ordinary in these Britons to ask for baptism at a time of crisis when death might well be imminent. Constantius makes one remark which may throw light on the matter. He says that it was the days of Lent and so the soldiers vied with one another in flocking to the grace of baptism on Easter Sunday.[18] But if the men had been pagan, the fact of its being Easter would have been beside the point. It would have meant little or nothing to them. Christians would indeed expect baptism at Easter, Pentecost, or perhaps Epiphany, but pagans would be baptised at the time when they were converted, irrespective of whether it was Easter or not.

I am inclined to conclude, then, that the army – or, rather, most of it, for some of the men in it were not baptised[19] – was already christian before Germanus fell in with it; and so it would appear to be the case that this was the levy of the neighbouring town or towns, not an assemblage of country-folk. As we have seen, the townsfolk tended to be christian and Latin-

[16] Jones, *The Later Roman Empire*, II.980f.
[17] *Vita*, § 17 (264,5).
[18] *Ibid.* (264,6).
[19] See *ibid.*, 264,14: *pars maior exercitus*. Were the remainder already baptised or were they obstinate pagans? The fact that Constantius considered that some men of the army were not baptised on this occasion may mean that a considerable number was not baptised.

speaking. On this occasion, unlike that on which he spoke to the Alan king, Goar, Germanus is not said to have made use of an interpreter. On the supposition accepted here, the difficulties and obscurities of the narrative appear to be somewhat less daunting than if we suppose that the army, when Germanus first encountered it, was composed of country-dwelling, Celtic-speaking, pagan peasants who were miraculously converted to christianity in a period of two or three days. Here the argument from silence cannot be ignored.

The christians, then, were townsfolk and villa-dwellers, and some of them lived *per deuia*, which does not prove that they were poor. Constantius describes the Pelagians who met Germanus in formal debate as rich and well dressed; but these were the heretics who lived in the centre of population – a town, presumably – where the debate took place. We do not know whether the rural Pelagians were equally well heeled: but what we know of Pelagians in general suggests that in many cases this was the fact. Indeed, they regarded it as a mark of plebeian vulgarity to think what everyone else thinks.[20] On the other hand, it is hard to believe that the Catholics were crushed by poverty or that they were dressed in rags. Since they were not peasants, *coloni*, slaves, and the like, then presumably they were town-dwellers to some extent, but probably most of them were landowners: there is no need to think that *all* rich men were heretics. But Constantius's description of the heretics at the great debate as 'rich and well dressed' would hardly have been very effective if the Catholics as a whole had been equally well dressed and no less rich. And yet it is certainly not easy to see that the difference between Catholic and Pelagian denoted a difference of class. The richer classes were probably divided on the subject, the bulk of them in this area having gone over to the heresy, whereas the poorer classes, especially the rural poor, were neither Catholic nor heretic, but pagan. The inference, no doubt, is that towards the middle of the fifth century Britain was still an overwhelmingly pagan country.

Another puzzling question is why in Constantius's account there was no British bishop, no British priest, on the scene. Was not the baptism of the army an act of gross interference by Germanus and Lupus in the diocesan affairs of another bishop? Indeed, why is there no reference in the *Vita* to bishops in Britain? The disappearance of the cities in that part of Britain (if they had disappeared – and archaeology shows that they are not likely to have done so)[21] cannot have entailed the disappearance of the bishops. Constantius is silent: why does he make no reference to British bishops at any part of his narrative? This is a nice illustration of the desperate inadequacy of our information. It is of the first importance to be clear that in §§ 17 and 26 *sacerdotes, sacerdotum*,[22] refer to Germanus and his companion-bishop, Severus,

---

[20] See Honorius's law printed in Migne, *Patrologia Latina*, XLVIII.381, 'insignem notam plebeiae aestimat uilitatis sentire cum cunctis', of Pelagius and Caelestius.

[21] See p. 10, n. 33, above.

[22] *Vita*, pp. 264.5, 270.6 & 12.

while in § 25 the phrase *preces sacerdotum omnium*[23] means the prayers of all the bishops of the relevant part of Gaul.[24] These phrases do not refer to British bishops. But if Germanus encountered no bishops in Britain, did not this fact itself call for comment and explanation? On the other hand, if Constantius, writing fifty or sixty years later, had no definite information on the matter, would he not inevitably have used the word *sacerdotes* or *episcopi* somewhere in the course of his narrative? It looks, then, as though he had – or thought that he had – definite information on the matter. Can it be that he omits reference to the subject because the bishops of this region of Britain had gone over to the Pelagians *en bloc*? In that case, why not report such a remarkable fact? At all events, we know that there were British bishops in the fourth century, and we know that there were British bishops in Gildas's day towards the middle of the sixth century: how then could there fail to have been British bishops in the fifth century? Indeed, St Patrick mentions British bishops in the very first section of his *Confession*. I should agree with Leslie Alcock that 'the absence of any mention of British bishops must represent an omission on the part of Germanus's biographer rather than any authentic historical fact'.[25] But why did the biographer omit to refer to them? If British bishops took part in the events of 429 without Constantius's knowing of their involvement, then his ignorance of the first British visit of St Germanus was even more profound than we could have guessed. I am tempted to think that the bishops, or the bishop, of the region of Britain in question had joined the heretics and that Constantius thought it discreet to suppress the fact: it would reflect no credit on the Church.

Otherwise, it would seem out of the question that Constantius suppressed the facts deliberately to glorify his hero. If one or more British bishops had put up a valiant though ineffective struggle against the heresy before Germanus arrived in the island, Constantius might well have given them their due credit. To be sure, it was his task to glorify Germanus, not some obscure British bishops living on the opposite shore of the Ocean. But if Germanus had succeeded in rebutting the heretics when the local bishops had failed, this would reflect credit on him. When towards the end of his story Constantius describes Germanus's visit to Ravenna, he does indeed mention that Peter (Chrysologus) was bishop there at the time,[26] but he says not a word about him except that when Germanus died Peter joined in the scramble to lay hands on the saint's possessions and managed to get away with his cowl and his hair-shirt.[27] What his relations were with the saint of

[23] *Ibid.*, § 25 (269,15); cf. § 27 (271,3).

[24] *Contra*, Grosjean, 'Notes', pp. 174 and 177, n. 1.

[25] Alcock, *Arthur's Britain*, p. 133, a judicious paragraph (although I cannot see the evidence for the charge of 'anti-Celtic prejudice' which he and others bring against Bede). When Johnson, *Later Roman Britain*, p. 110, writes that Germanus 'met civic leaders, church dignitaries, and much of the outward trappings of normal Roman life', I am not sure which passage of Constantius's *Vita* he has in mind.

[26] *Vita*, § 35 (276,11).

[27] *Ibid.*, § 43 (281,15).

Auxerre, whether he assisted his mission, what he thought of him, what impression Peter made on Germanus, and so on – of all this Constantius says not a word. His business is with Germanus and Germanus only. Yet Peter with his golden words was far more eminent than any beleaguered British bishop of the fifth century, facing simultaneously heresy and barbarians. On the whole, I find it hard to believe that Constantius would have said nothing whatever of the British bishops who fought against heresy, if there had been any such.

If he were prepared to say nothing about the Britons who opposed Pelagianism in their island – and he must have believed that such men existed, for who else would have sent the delegation to Gaul? – it is not likely that he would as much as breathe the name of Agricola. All that has been recorded about him is contained in that single entry in Prosper's invaluable *Chronicle*, § 1301.[28] It may well have been he who introduced Pelagianism into Britain. Although Pelagius himself was a Briton, there is no trace of his heretical doctrines in his native land in the first decade of the fifth century. Nor could there be: Pelagius's teachings were not considered to be heretical until the Council of Carthage met in 411, and St Augustine did not begin the long series of his writings against the heretic until 412.[29] Yet some British scholars appear to think that far-sighted British theologians of a political cast of mind not only grasped the implications of Pelagius's teachings but actually formed political 'parties' to uphold or oppose those teachings before 410. *Before 410!* That is to say, they did so some years before the dull-witted St Augustine of Hippo was able to grasp that Pelagius's teachings were unorthodox! And these British theologians – or should we call them 'clair-voyants'? – attached themselves respectively to anti-Roman and pro-Roman parties. We are told of 'the *inimici gratiae*, the party of independence which had thrown out the *gratiosi* and officials of the old régime in the days of Constantine III'.[30] It is necessary only to state these theories, while bearing in mind the chronology of Pelagius's career, to see that they are untenable. We have no evidence for the existence of Pelagian heretics in Britain until Agricola appeared on the scene in the 420s. I should accept the view of Charles Thomas that 'the orthodox reaction [viz, the appeal to Gaul for help] arose understandably immediately there seemed to be any chance of heretical ideas getting out of hand'.[31]

Was Agricola a Briton or was he a Pelagian propagandist who had come to

---

[28] Mommsen, *Chronica Minora*, I.472.

[29] On the chronology of Pelagius and his ideas see de Plinval, *Pélage*, p. 207.

[30] Myres, 'Pelagius', especially pp. 31 and 35, who nevertheless admits (p. 22) that Pelagius in the years 394–410 was 'a sincere and forceful teacher without apparently attracting any serious ecclesiastical misgivings'. How then did it come about that the Britons were divided before 410 on the heresy of Pelagius? It would be tedious and pointless to list those who have been misled by this style of argument and who speak of 'romanising and insular parties', the one orthodox in religion, the other heretical, contending in early fifth-century Britain, or of 'a powerful Pelagian party in Britain, anti-Roman in sentiment'. Such fancies are rightly discarded by Alcock, *Arthur's Britain*, p. 100.

[31] Thomas, *Christianity*, p. 56.

21

the island from overseas, perhaps after being exiled from Gaul or Italy? If he was a Briton, then his father Severianus is one of the few British bishops of this period whom we know by name. At any rate, the father, too, was a Pelagian. It is not wholly certain that the son introduced the heresy into Britain, but it certainly was newly arrived there when Agricola first makes his appearance in our sources in the 420s.[32] It was an extraordinary feat on his part to have propagated his doctrines successfully after the triple condemnation of them in 418 – by the Emperor, by the pope, and by a council of 214 bishops meeting at Carthage.[33] Further harsh political measures followed in 419, 421, and 425, to say nothing of the condemnations by other councils and by no fewer than four popes in all.[34] Although support for Pelagius on the Continent by no means died out immediately after 418, it necessarily went to some extent underground. There heretics were outside the law, but they were not in all cases afraid to publish. Yet to launch out, as Agricola did, on an aggressive campaign of public preaching and of public proselytising – and above all to do so with success – was perhaps only possible in a land where the Emperor's power could no longer silence him. What became of him we do not know. Did he live to debate with Germanus in 429? If so, did he survive his defeat (if he *was* defeated) and help to build up his doctrines among the Britons to an extent which made a second visit by Germanus a necessity some years later? No one can tell. What a happy position it would be if only we could receive some further information about this Agricola, who propagated heretical ideas in Britain, in exchange for some of our knowledge of the dreary military Agricola of the Flavian period, whose only claims to fame are the gallons of blood which he shed and the fact that he contrived to marry his daughter to Cornelius Tacitus!

We know nothing of the efforts which the British Catholics had made to defeat Agricola and the heretics before they appealed to Gaul; but we can say of them with assurance that they were dismally unsuccessful. The Catholics must have been facing a heavy defeat when they appealed to the Gallic bishops. It was not quite an unheard-of action in the West for the Catholics of an entire political diocese – or what had once been a diocese – to admit their inadequacy as openly as the British Catholics did in 429, for the Britons had already done the same thing at the beginning of the century when they brought over Victricius, bishop of Rouen, to unravel their problems at that time.[35] But we never hear of such a thing anywhere in the West outside Britain. We never hear, for example, that the Spanish bishops were obliged to send to Gaul for help against Priscillianism even at the height of the raids of the Sueves in their country.

It would be a mistake to exaggerate the success of the heretics. We must not forget, for example, that Gildas, writing only about a century later,

[32] *Ibid.*
[33] So de Plinval, *Pélage*, p. 323f.
[34] *Ibid.*, p. 345f.
[35] Victricius of Rouen, *De Laude Sanctorum*, in Migne, *Patrologia Latina*, XX.443–58.

knows nothing at all about Pelagius and his teachings or those struggles in Britain between heresy and orthodoxy.[36]

Constantius tells us lamentably little about the state of religion in Britain over and above what we learn from that single priceless entry in Prosper's *Chronicle*. True, he tells us of the second visit of Germanus to the island in the company of a certain Severus. But he says nothing about Severus, who as a result is only a name to us, although Bede claims to know something of him. Constantius does not tell us the date of this second visit, and we have seen what difficulties we should find ourselves in if we had to deduce from his narrative the date of the first visit.[37] In the case of the second visit the difficulties are hardly less baffling. He does not tell us what had brought British Pelagianism back to life at the time of the second visit (if indeed it had ever become moribund). He says that Pelagianism was again spreading in Britain, although there were only a few teachers and leaders.[38] We may suspect that Constantius has seriously understated the facts here, for if there had been only a few champions of Pelagianism the Britons might well have been able to deal with the situation by themselves. The fact that they had once more to ask for help from Gaul suggests that something of a crisis, something which was no detail, had arisen once again. But what happened during the second visit was almost wholly unknown to Constantius apart from the miraculous cure of the lame son of Elafius.

Even apart from the second visit Constantius's ignorance of British affairs is at first sight surprising. Of paganism in the island he can say nothing, or at any rate does not choose to say anything. Of Church-organisation in Britain he is either ignorant or else thinks that any reference to the subject was irrelevant to his story. (If he thought the general condition of the Church in Britain to be of no interest to his readers, we need not be surprised to find that he has nothing to say about the condition of the Church in Ireland, where dramatic events were taking place at this very time or at any rate in 431.) Constantius refers neither to the cities nor to the villas of Britain nor to the religion of either. Indeed, of British life his ignorance or his indifference or both could hardly be more complete. Prosper gives us in five lines of the printed text more 'hard' information about the ecclesiastical position in Britain than Constantius is able to convey, or chooses to convey, in many pages. Yet where Constantius speaks of Gaul and Italy he is all but impeccable.[39] He is rarely open to criticism when he deals with the Continent. Nora Chadwick remarked, 'When we reflect that Constantius was not primarily composing with a historical end in view, the amount of historical matter which he records is more striking than his omissions or inaccuracies'.[40] That is true of his Gallic and Italian chapters. It is not true of his British

---

[36] Thompson, 'Gildas', p. 211f. Yet Gildas quotes (unwittingly, as I think) a sentence from a Pelagian writer. See *De Excidio*, II.38, with Thompson, loc. cit.
[37] See p. 2 above.
[38] *Vita*, §25 (269,15).
[39] But see p. 70 below.
[40] Chadwick, *Poetry and Letters*, p. 262.

chapters. Why? It is not easy to resist the conclusion that he says little of Britain because he knows little about it.

How gladly we should give his one fifth-century British personal name, that of Elafius, in exchange for an exact description of the appointment which he held (if he held any official appointment) or for the name of the place where Elafius encountered the saint! But that is a relative detail. Even on the basic question – was Britain a christian or a pagan country? – Constantius has nothing to say. There were many christians in Britain, to be sure; but that is a different matter. Most surprising of all, however, is that of Pelagianism itself and its teachings Constantius appears to know little or nothing. There was a clash between orthodoxy and the heresy in Britain at this date. But what form did the clash take? What were the issues at stake? In this connexion Constantius's account of the great debate could not possibly be less informative. And how could a single debate between Germanus and the leading heretics resolve these issues? Constantius may have known the answers to these questions but, if so, he did not think it important to give his readers the slightest hint at their nature. Can we be certain that he knew what the teachings of Pelagius amounted to? It may be the case that he knew as little about the theology of his day as did his friend Sidonius Apollinaris. It is not certain that Constantius was a priest;[41] and, even if he was ordained, his theological knowledge, like that of Sidonius, may have been decidedly limited.[42] The *Life* is a tract which aims at commemorating Germanus: it is not a polemical tract directed against the teachings of Pelagius or even at upholding the position of the orthodox where it differed from the position of the heretics.

Prosper reports one remarkable fact which he can hardly be suspected of inventing. It is that Pope Celestine sent Germanus to Britain 'as his vicar', *uice sua*, his 'representative'. In the Late Roman period, the popes appointed papal vicars from time to time in order to deal with important or urgent problems which called for swift and decisive action on the spot and which could not await the long delays of communication with Rome. But in two ways the appointment of Germanus as vicar was exceptional. In the first place, this was the only occasion, as far as we know, when a pope sent his vicar to Britain. Indeed, it was the first occasion on which a pope is recorded to have sent out a bishop *uice sua* to any place. And it was almost the only occasion when a bishop was appointed vicar from another province than that in which had arisen the problem which he was appointed to resolve (although in 508 Caesarius of Arles was vicar not only in Gaul but also in Spain). But we have no hint either in Prosper or in Constantius at the precise nature of the crisis which demanded this unusual remedy. We can only infer that it was important and that it was urgent. And Constantius stresses that help from Gaul was a matter of urgency: it must be sent 'as quickly as

[41] See p. 78 below.
[42] Stevens, *Sidonius*, p. 131f.

possible', *quam primum*.[43] It is clear that we must, later on, examine in detail our two accounts of how Germanus came to visit Britain in 429.[44]

As for the immediate reason for sending Germanus across the sea, we can only guess. We might assume that, directly before 429, Agricola or one of his supporters had managed to win an important and dramatic success. Suppose, for example, that the bulk of the inhabitants of a major diocese under the leadership of its bishop had suddenly decided to go over *en bloc* to Pelagianism: would not the appointment of a papal vicar from overseas be a wise step for the pope to take? That, to be sure, is only one possibility out of many; but it shows the *sort* of crisis which might have arisen.

Here are some interesting remarks by J. B. Bury.[45]

When many of the Western provinces had wholly or partly passed out of the Emperor's control, it was a matter of importance to strive to keep alive the idea of the Empire and the old attachment to Rome in the minds of the provincials. . . . The day might come when it would be possible to recover some of these lost lands, which the Imperial government never acknowledged to be really lost, and in the meantime a close ecclesiastical unity presented itself as a powerful means for preserving the bonds of sentiment, which would then prove an indispensable help. To accustom the churches in Gaul and Britain, Spain and Africa to look up to Rome and refer their disputes and difficulties to the Roman bishop was a wise policy from the secular point of view, and it was doubtless principally by urging considerations of this nature that Leo was able to induce the government to establish the supremacy of his see.

It should be observed that these ideas, interesting as they are, are the ideas of J. B. Bury. There is no evidence that any one of them ever penetrated the heads of Valentinian III or of Pope Leo the Great. No doubt they ought to have done so. Indeed, they *may* have done so; but there is no evidence that they did so in fact.

However that may be, we must feel neither joy nor sorrow that Pelagianism was defeated in Britain, as elsewhere. 'The Pelagians were Late Roman men', writes Peter Brown, 'to a depressing extent. For them, as for everyone else in that age of absolutism, reform meant only one thing: reform from the top; yet more laws, sanctioned by yet more horrific punishments.'[46] It is not easy to feel any deep emotion when Tweedledum defeats Tweedledee.

[43] *Vita*, § 12 (259,7).
[44] See p. 79f. below.
[45] Bury, *A History*, I.365.
[46] Brown, 'Pelagius', p. 111 = *Religion and Society*, p. 204.

IV

GOVERNMENT

It is astonishing to notice throughout Constantius's narrative of both visits to Britain how little the British political authorities interfered with the Gallic bishops, either to help or to hinder their work. On each visit a Briton of authority or wealth or at any rate of prominence made his appearance and asked the visiting bishops to cure his child; but on neither occasion did the personages in question or any other man of power show any interest whatever in the purpose of the bishops' presence. If they did so, Constantius thought their intervention to be of less interest than the story of the miraculous cure of the two children. But in fact it is hardly conceivable that he would have omitted, had the tradition on which he was drawing not omitted, to mention the hero's relations with the ruling powers if he had had any: Constantius is very emphatic in describing Germanus's relations with the rulers of Gaul and Italy.

The supporters of Pelagius in Britain at the time of the first visit were rich men, *conspicui diuitiis, ueste fulgentes*,[1] but Constantius gives no hint about their relationship with the 'man of tribunician power'. The latter had apparently taken no part in the debate on Pelagianism; and indeed the entire debate on religion seems quite clearly to have gone on independently of him. He appeared on the scene only after the Pelagians had been routed; or at any rate it was only then that he came forward out of the crowd, *procedit in medium*.[2] He may have been listening to the debate, but there is no hint that he had once been a heretic or indeed that he was now a Catholic. He is not represented as having any contact with either religious party. He and his wife were delighted by the miraculous cure of their blind daughter: but Constantius does not claim that the incident led to their conversion to Catholicism.[3] For all Constantius says, they might have been pagans. Again, the prominent man who appears in the narrative of the second visit, Elafius, was among those who were waiting for the visitors to arrive in Britain, but he was not waiting so as to inform them about the condition of the Church or the attitude of the

---

[1] *Vita*, § 14 (261,9).
[2] *Ibid.*, § 15 (261,23).
[3] *Ibid.* (262,8). I do not think that the laudatory sentence which follows (262,9–11) necessarily contradicts this statement.

government. He was there to ask them to cure his son.[4] There is no hint that he had any interest in the problems of heresy and orthodoxy.

According to Constantius, the organisers of both visits had not even given advance notice to the prominent men of Britain about the invitation which they had sent to Gaul or about the Gallic bishops' arrival. We are explicitly told that Elafius heard of the bishops' arrival through rumour and through no other agency;[5] he had certainly not helped to organise the visit. And on the first visit, too, the bishops were welcomed by a 'multitude' who had heard of their impending arrival (*uenturos*) by rumour.[6] On neither occasion did the secular authorities (whoever they may have been) reveal any interest whatsoever in the safe arrival of the visitors or in welcoming them ashore or in the course of the sectarian debate or in the outcome of the sectarian struggle. This last point is most unexpected and is not at all easy to parallel. Where else in the Western world at this date was heresy a matter of indifference to christian rulers? How could christian authorities possibly have been uninterested in an issue which, as Prosper tells us, the pope himself had regarded with grave concern? True, the authorities' lack of interest is based on an argument from silence:[7] since Constantius does not mention that they were present at the debate and took part in it, *therefore* they were not present and took no part. But the argument must not be questioned on that account. It would have been a wonderful triumph for Germanus if he had won over the doubting king or the heretical tyrant, and Constantius would certainly not have omitted to describe any such victory if he knew that it had been scored. Nor is it likely that he would have omitted to say so if Germanus had been mixing on equal terms with kings or tyrants or other great ones. As I have mentioned, he is by no means reticent about the saint's relations with the Praetorian Prefect of Gaul or with the Imperial family in Italy.

Constantius regards the first visit as an unqualified success (although we may have some reservations, seeing that in the end a second visit turned out to be necessary). But if the local king or tyrant had put in an appearance at the debate and had not been convinced by the visitors, Constantius might have had some difficulty in claiming unqualified victory for his hero. We must never forget that his primary aim is to glorify the saint: and yet in this connexion he says nothing. He makes no claims. There is not the slightest reason to think that the political authorities helped or hindered the British Catholics or the British Pelagians or that they were in any way enlightened by the Gallic bishops' visit. Throughout the entire sequence of events during both of Germanus's visits, the British rulers are simply not there. Of all the oddities of the history of Britain at this time none is more surprising than this.

[4] *Vita*, § 26 (270,1).
[5] *Ibid.*
[6] *Ibid.*, § 13 (260,19f.).
[7] See p. 4 above.

27

Another astonishing fact recorded about the second visit to Britain is the fate of the defeated Pelagians: they were sent into exile by the church-congregation which had been listening to the debate between the champions of Catholicism and those of Pelagianism, *omniumque sententia prauitatis auctores expulsi insula.*[8] Where else in the Roman world, or in what had until recently been the Roman world, could a preacher's congregation send men into exile? Where else could civilians exile men because they thought them to be heretics?[9] Whatever form of government existed in this place, it is hardly possible to believe that the two overseas bishops, almost total strangers to the area, could have inflicted this punishment on natives of a realm to which they were, by invitation, paying a short and private visit. Any attempt to interfere with the inhabitants' rights and even with their personal freedom would, one might expect, have attracted the unpleasant attention of whatever political authorities there may have been in the region. And yet the sentence of exile was not passed by any local political authorities, as far as Constantius knew or reported. Again, if the local authorities had sided with the Catholics, it is hard to believe that Constantius would have omitted to say so. Indeed, it is hard to believe that the heretics would ever have won such dramatic successes as to justify the words *in populo quem subuerterant.*[10] Borius understandably cannot accept this state of affairs and supposes that the sentence of exile was due to the political authority, doubtless (he thinks) represented by Elafius;[11] but Constantius gives us not the faintest hint that this was so, and it seems impossible to think of any reason why he would have suppressed it if it had been the case. What the text of the *Vita* tells us is that the champions of the heresy were made over to the bishops to be transferred abroad *omnium sententia.*[12] If we can press those words, it looks as though the bishops' audience rose up at the end of the sermon and on the spot condemned the heretics to exile. And indeed during the first visit the crowd at the end of the debate with the Pelagians had some difficulty in refraining from laying violent hands on the heretics.[13]

It is difficult to study this matter without recalling that law which Honorius enacted on 30 April 418 and which has survived although it never found a place in the Theodosian Code. In this law the Emperor decreed that men who were found anywhere in the act of conferring about the crime of Pelagianism were liable to be arrested by anyone whatsover, brought to a public hearing, accused by anybody without distinction, sentenced, and

[8] *Vita*, § 27 (270,19).
[9] Something of a parallel has been recorded from Spain. In 448 Antoninus, bishop of Merida, arrested a Manichaean and without reference to the civil authorities caused him to be expelled from the province of Lusitania: Hydatius, *Chronicon*, § 138 (ed. Mommsen, *Chronica Minora*, II.25).
[10] *Vita*, § 14 (261,10).
[11] Borius, *Constance*, p. 88.
[12] *Vita*, § 27 (270,19).
[13] *Ibid.*, § 14 (261,22).

condemned to inexorable exile.[14] But the British Pelagians had been doing precisely what this law prohibits when they debated with Germanus, and they met the punishment which the law prescribes. Is it possible that the Britons of this region had heard of Honorius's legislation? In fact, was Roman law still enforced in this part of the island? The abolition of Roman law had certainly and explicitly been one of the main achievements of the rebels of 409;[15] and it would be a bold man who would assert that Roman legislation of 418 could have been enforced in Britain in the 430s or 440s. The Gallic bishops, of course, would have recognised the validity of Honorius's laws. Our question is whether those laws were recognised in Britain in practice if not in theory, on occasion if not always, in some places if not in others. It seems more than unlikely, and we must conclude that although Pelagian belief was outlawed and illegal on the Continent and in Africa it was perfectly legal in Britain. British Catholics might resent this freedom: there is no reason to think that British governments did so.

In fact, we have some further evidence on this exiling of the Pelagians (although I have not been able to find a discussion of it in this connexion); and this further evidence, so far from elucidating the matter, throws it into even greater confusion than Constantius had left it in, and – worse still – causes us to feel doubts (if we did not feel them before) about the value of Constantius himself as a source of historical information about Britain. We learn from Prosper of Aquitaine, though not from his *Chronicle*, that Pope Celestine, who died in July 432, freed the British provinces from the infection of heresy 'since he shut out from that remote place in the Ocean some enemies of grace who had seized upon the soil of their birth-place'; that is to say, the pope exiled some Pelagians from Britain, the land in which Pelagius had been born.[16] Now, this work of Prosper's dates from 433/4, very soon after the death of Pope Celestine; and it presumably refers to some incident in the activities of Germanus, for Germanus is the only known representative of the pope to have visited Britain about this time. The passage, then, must refer to Germanus's first visit to Britain and not to his second which on any chronology still lay in the future when Prosper wrote those words. The meaning probably is that Germanus, the pope's vicar, had exiled by the authority of the pope some heretics from Britain in 429. But this is not at all what Constantius tells us. Constantius speaks of heretics being exiled in

---

[14] Migne, *Patrologia Latina*, XLVIII.385, 'hos ergo repertos ubicumque de hoc tam infando scelere conferentes a quibuscumque iubemus corripi, deductosque ad audientiam publicam promiscue ab omnibus accusari, ita ut probationem conuicti criminis stilus publicus insequatur, ipsis inexorate exilii deportatione damnatis'. On the meaning of *stilus publicus* here Migne's notes mention that *stilus = sententia*: cf. *Codex Theodosianus*, IX.42,15, 'si quis posthac stilum, quod absit, proscriptionis exceperit'; and XVI.5,57, '[Montanistae] stilum deportationis excipiant'.
[15] See p. 32 below.
[16] Prosper, *Contra Collatorem*, § 21 (ed. Migne, *Patrologia Latina*, LI.271), 'nec uero segniore cura ab hoc eodem morbo Britannias liberauit, quando quosdam inimicos gratiae solum suae originis occupantes etiam ab illo secreto exclusit Oceani, et ordinato Scotis episcopo dum romanam insulam studet seruare catholicam fecit etiam barbaram christianam'.

connexion with the *second* visit, which took place when Celestine was some years in his grave. Also, he ascribes the exile of the heretics, not to Germanus acting on the authority of the pope, but to the congregation which had been listening to Germanus. It can hardly be doubted – if Constantius and Prosper are referring to the same event – that the story as told by Prosper (such as it is) is decidedly more plausible than that of Constantius. We might of course suppose that Pelagians had been exiled on both occasions, the exiles of 429 being ordered by Celestine and those of the second visit being imposed spontaneously by the British Catholics.[17] But why should Constantius once again be ignorant of the actions of the pope? He evidently did not know that it was the pope who had sent Germanus to Britain:[18] now he does not know that Germanus was acting in the pope's name when he exiled the British Pelagians, or at any rate some of them, in 429.

The exiling of the heretics is not the last of our problems in this connexion. The convicted men were made over to the two Gallic bishops to be carried off *ad mediterranea*. The phrase in its context would naturally mean, 'into the interior of Britain'. But in that same sentence in which the phrase occurs, Constantius says that the heretics' leaders 'were expelled from the island', *expulsi insula*.[19] At first sight it is tempting to accept the view that the bishops were on an island – say, the Isle of Wight or of Thanet[20] – that the Pelagians were expelled from that island, and that the bishops thereupon carried them off into the interior of Britain. That hypothesis might explain the language of this sentence, and it would also solve some of our other problems. If we suppose that the Gallic bishops' activities were confined to an island, we need not worry about the absence of place-names and the like: if Constantius knew of any, they would have been meaningless to his readers. We need not worry about the absence of references to *urbes* and the like: the travellers came to none of any consequence. We need not wonder why Constantius mentions no officials: in this area none of any importance made his appearance at the relevant time. In the Isle of Wight there would have been rich and well dressed men with plenty of flunkeys to follow them around.

But there are insuperable objections to any such theory as that the bishops visited, not the mainland of Britain, but an island off the British coast. If a Roman writer, speaking of visitors to Britain, mentions that certain persons

[17] It may not be irrelevant in this connexion to notice some words of Gratian's law of 378/9, *Collectio Avellana*, XIII.12: 'si in longinquioribus partibus alicuius ferocitas talis emerserit, omnis eius causae dictio ad metropolitani in eadem prouincia episcopi deducatur examen, uel, si ipse metropolitanus est, Romam necessario uel ad eos, quos romanus episcopus iudices dederit, sine relatione contendat, ita tamen ut, quicunque deiecti sunt, ab eius tantum urbis finibus segregentur, in quibus fuerint sacerdotes'. Was there a metropolitan bishop among Germanus's opponents in Britain? We could well understand the alarm of the pope and the Gallic bishops if it had been reported to them that a metropolitan bishop of a crucially important diocese had gone over to the heretics. Such an emergency would account excellently for the mission of Germanus; and such an explanation of the events would show the pope exercising his powers outside the frontiers of the Roman empire.

[18] See p. 79 below.

[19] *Vita*, § 27 (270,20).

[20] For the Isle of Wight, see Grosjean, 'Notes', p. 176f.

30

were banished from the *insula* and leaves that word without further quali-
fication, he must certainly be taken to mean 'Britain' itself rather than some
island, lying off the coast of Britain, which he has not mentioned hitherto. We
are obliged to conclude that the condemned Pelagians were banished from
Britain and sent to the interior of Gaul, though it has to be admitted that to
take *ad mediterranea* here as meaning the 'interior of Gaul' is almost as harsh
as to take *insula* to mean some island other than Britain itself. Either interpretation involves accusing Constantius of uncharacteristically bad writing.
And the matter is not made easier to understand by the fact that not many
years previously, in 425, the Emperors had banished Pelagian bishops from
Gaul! (They had banished them from Rome in 418.[21]) To import a new batch
of Pelagians into Gaul in 429 or later would hardly have been the best way in
which to win the regard of Valentinian III.

But the major reason for holding that the narrative of the first visit to
Britain cannot relate only or mainly to an island off the south coast is this.
The first mission of Germanus was not ordered only by a large synod (*synodus
numerosa*)[22] of the Gallic bishops. As we shall see, it was ordered by the pope
himself, and Germanus travelled to Britain as the papal vicar, *papa Caelestinus
Germanum . . . uice sua mittit*, as Prosper says. It is hardly likely that even a
Gallic synod, to say nothing of the pope, would have worried very much if
Pelagianism had corrupted little more than a small island off the coast. And
indeed Prosper remarks that Agricola corrupted, not just one town, but 'the
Churches of Britain', *ecclesias Britanniae*, a phrase which would seem to
indicate a substantial number of the ecclesiastical dioceses of the island, or at
the least a substantial proportion of the city- and villa-dwelling inhabitants;
and this is confirmed by the lament of the British delegation to Gaul in 429
that the Pelagians 'had seized upon the peoples far and wide', *late populos
occupasse*.[23] True, the phrases in both cases are rhetorical and may well be an
overstatement.[24] But beyond any doubt Pelagian successes had been extensive
and far from negligible. In at least one region of Britain the heresy had made
substantial headway among the richer classes. On the other hand, we must
not forget that Gildas, writing only about a century later, says nothing at all
about Pelagius and his teachings.[25] The heretical doctrine's success, that is to
say, was probably confined to a limited, but not a negligible, part of
Britain.[26] There were areas to which Pelagianism had not penetrated; but
where it had penetrated it had won a frightening number of adherents –
frightening, that is, to the pope and the Gallic bishops. The visiting bishops
were not concerned with some fringe-area of the island but with a region

---

[21] *Constitutiones Sirmondianae*, §6, of 9 July 425, addressed to the Praetorian Prefect of Gaul.
[22] *Vita*, §12 (259,7).
[23] *Ibid.*
[24] See p. 81 below.
[25] See p. 22 above.
[26] I am convinced that if Gildas had known of a British heresy he would have mentioned it.
See Thompson, 'Gildas', p. 211f.

important enough for its defection from Catholicism to be of concern to the pope himself far away in Italy.

Clearly, the absence of any visible form of government in the important region visited by Germanus, together with the exile of the leading Pelagians without struggle or protest, presents us with problems of baffling obscurity. What makes the position even more difficult to understand is that the leading heretics were rich men, well dressed and accompanied by numbers of fawning toadies. Hence they were precisely the sort of person whom we should expect to find closely associated with whatever government existed in that region at that date. Yet no government stepped in to support them, and although they escaped violence in 429 – as far as Constantius was aware – they or some of them were forced into exile on the second visit. What the *Vita* describes seems to be a land from which the Roman administration has wholly disappeared and in which, apart from the indifferent man of tribunician power, nothing very obvious has taken its place.

I should suggest that any government which could disregard the pope's anxiety and could ignore his representative when he was present in their dominions could not be a government of militant Catholics. That, at least, is hardly open to debate or question. But it is equally difficult to see how that government could have been made up of Pelagians. Would not a Pelagian government have interfered with the visitors from Gaul, or at any rate could it possibly have remained neutral and unmoved and out of sight when Germanus went to work against its beliefs and preached against its supporters with success? Would such a government have allowed him to preach openly without the slightest attempt to silence him? Above all, would it have permitted him to send some of its citizens into exile? If so, it was the most liberal government ever to appear in the ancient christian world! All such questions must, of course, be answered in the negative; and there is only one hypothesis – as far as I can see – which will account for the facts. The situation described by Constantius can be explained only if we suppose that the rulers of this part of Britain at this date were not christians at all, whether orthodox or heretical, but pagans.

That the rulers of some part of southern Britain may have been pagan at this time will come as a surprise only to those who have misinterpreted the events of 409. In 409 the Britons, or some of them, had risen in revolt against the Roman government (whether that was then directed, as far as Britain was concerned, by Honorius or by Constantine III, then still a usurper), had expelled the Roman administrators, civil and military, had abolished the use of Roman law, and had seceded from the Roman empire.[27] The question arises as to which Britons made this unique move. Who rebelled, and why did they do so? It would be a blunder to suppose that the richest classes, the great landowners, carried out such a policy. The Roman empire was run, and

---

[27] Thompson, 'Zosimus', pp. 455–9. There is no reason to think that Honorius's letter was a rescript, that is, a reply to a letter which the Britons had sent to him.

always had been run, in the interests of the large landowners.[28] For the great landowners to leave voluntarily the organisation which had hitherto prevented any threat to their ownership of their estates would have been inconceivable. The *curiales*, too, although their complaints were loud and many, were prosperous enough under the rule of the later Emperors.[29] But they made the lives of many poor men intolerable. *Quot curiales, tot tyranni*, cried Salvian, writing *ca* 440/1. And apart from their relative economic prosperity they ranked as *honestiores* and so were in theory more or less exempt from the death-penalty and from judicial torture.[30] Again, the first military action of the British rebels was to free the *ciuitates* (or *poleis*, as Zosimus calls them) from the Saxon raiders of that year.[31] Accordingly, there are those who think that since the rebels made it their first task to free the 'cities' (as they render *poleis*), therefore they must have been the city-dwellers. But to this thesis there are objections. In the first place, it is difficult to believe that the urban population was adequate in numbers or in organisation to undertake the momentous task of seceding from Rome. And even if an adequate urban population existed, it could hardly have carried with it a very large proportion of the rest of the inhabitants of the area in question – I mean, a large enough number to put an effective army in the field and to supply it there. Secondly, the town-dwellers had no motive for secession. They were taxed, but on nothing like the scale of the rural poor. Thirdly, it cannot be supposed that the Saxon invaders began their raid in 409 with the improbable step of beleaguering the walled cities of Britain.[32] Siege-warfare was beyond the powers of the Germanic peoples, even of peoples more advanced by far than the Saxons – the Goths, for instance. And of this inability the Germans themselves were well aware. That on this occasion the Saxons, who cannot have been well supplied with food,[33] should start their operations in Britain by undertaking a series of sieges, which they knew from the outset to be hopeless, is improbable. And we may recall that the Saxons of 429 were trying to bring the British forces to battle:[34] they did not sit feebly down in front of the local city which they knew that they could not possibly reduce if it was walled. In other words, it is a mistake to translate *poleis* in Zosimus, VI.5,3, as 'cities'. What Zosimus means to tell us in connexion with the events of 409 is that the *ciuitates* of Britain, the 'states' or rather the 'city-states', were menaced by the barbarians, that is to say, simply that

[28] Jones, *The Later Roman Empire*, I.357–65. On the other hand, Hanson, 'The date', p. 72, is inclined to think that the British aristocracy initiated the move for independence; and Frere, *Britannia*, p. 410, holds that it was the curial class which rose 'in the interests of the towns'. But in what way would secession advance the interests of the towns? I find it difficult to accept that the prosperous classes, or those who were relatively prosperous, would ever have dreamed of seceding: The most which we might expect of them is that they should set up a usurping emperor of their own.

[29] Jones, *The Later Roman Empire*, I.362–5, II.748–57.

[30] Salvian, *De Gubernatione Dei*, V.18.

[31] Zosimus, *History*, VI.5,3.

[32] The ineffectiveness of the Germans in siege-warfare is discussed by Thompson, *The Early Germans*, pp. 131–40.

[33] See p. 96 below.

[34] See p. 40 below.

various regions of the island were overrun by the invaders. In 409 there was an extensive invasion. Zosimus certainly does not mean that Britain was studded with besieged cities. He means that the British rebels began to clear the various affected regions of their intruders.

The only reasonable explanation of the secession of 409 is that it was carried through by the poorer classes in the countryside. These were the persons who had every reason to rebel. A recent scholar has written: 'In the palmiest days of the *pax romana* the life of the humblest peasants was one of utter drudgery, desperate poverty and severe oppression. The only thing to be said in its favour is that, for many, it was mercifully brief.'[35] The year 409 was not among the palmiest days of the Empire, but it brought one ray of sunshine: as far as we know, it was the first time, since the Claudian conquest of Britain in the first century A.D., when there were few or no effective armed forces of the Imperial government in the island. We could perhaps suppose that the rural poor had been waiting for this moment, but we cannot think that the town-dwellers or the moderately rich or the very rich landowners had been watching for such an opportunity: they had no compelling motive either in 409 or at any other time to secede or to look forward to a time when they could attempt to secede.

If we wish, we may call these rural rebels '*Bacaudae*'. Collingwood saw that the similarities between the social condition of Gaul and Spain, on the one hand, and that of Britain, on the other, were such that the existence of Bacaudae in Britain could be inferred from their existence and activities in Spain and Gaul.[36] What brought the Bacaudae into existence is no mystery: the main cause of the disaffection of the rural poor was the severity of the taxes and the corrupt methods of the tax-collectors and also the skill of the rich landowners in obliging the rural poor to pay the landowners' taxes as well as their own. 'The entire expenditure of the empire, the cost of feeding and clothing the army and civil service, the maintenance of the public transport system, and upkeep of the court and the food supply of the two capitals, with the single exception of the donative to the troops, was entirely borne by agriculture.'[37] Those who would convince us, then, that there were no rural-poor rebels in Britain at this date will begin no doubt by showing that the taxes were lower in the British provinces than elsewhere in the Gallic Prefecture and that the British tax-collectors were more kind-hearted, more gentlemanly, and less corrupt than their counterparts in the rest of the prefecture. Unhappily, it may prove difficult to find evidence to support either of these two patriotic but improbable propositions.

But since the term 'British Bacaudae' is regarded as an offensive one and has

---

[35] Todd, *Studies*, pp. 204–5.

[36] Collingwood [& Myres], *Roman Britain*, p. 303f.

[37] Jones, *The Later Roman Empire*, I,465. Note Salvian, *De Gubernatione Dei*, IV.30: 'inueniuntur tamen plurimi diuitum, quorum tributa pauperes ferunt, hoc est, inueniuntur plurimi diuitum, quorum tributa pauperes necant. Et quod inueniri dicimus plurimos, timeo ne uerius diceremus omnes.' On what caused Bacaudae to come into existence, there is no need to look further than *ibid.*, V.24–6. For recent writings on the Bacaudae see Thompson, *Romans and Barbarians*, p. 221f. See further Jones, *The Later Roman Empire*, I.457f., 467f.; de Ste. Croix, *The Class Struggle*, p. 497f.

34

aroused resentment and anger in some breasts, let us refrain from using it. Let us say instead that the revolt of 409 was carried through by slaves, *coloni*, tenant-farmers, peasants, army-deserters,[38] and other poor men aided by an occasional professional man (like that Eudoxius, a physician of Gaul, who fled to the Huns in 448), and even some persons who were by no means humbly born.[39] The revolt and the secession were an escape from the crushing, stifling burden of taxation. For such men as these, to leave the Roman *societas* would be no breach with tradition, no sentimental break with the golden past. A recent authority has put it succinctly: 'For them the collapse of the central administration spelled release, not deprivation'.[40] And there is one fact about the Britons in the early fifth century of which we may be certain: they were not so frightened of new ideas and even new practices as are some of those who study them in the later twentieth century. For example, we are told that the Gratian whom the Britons – a different kind of rebel in this case from those of 409 – elevated to the purple in 407 was 'the only usurper in the history of the Empire who was described as *municeps*'.[41] Or again, the Britons were the first people who are known to have seceded from the Roman Empire in the West, an unimaginably courageous and adventurous step into the unknown. The early fifth-century Britons certainly did not shrink from originality in thought and action.

According to our source of information, the British rebels declared their independence of Rome and abolished the use of Roman law. Their example was at once followed by the Armoricans and other Gauls.[42] Bearing in mind that Armorica extended as far east as the Seine[43] and that the rebels may have included people living even to the east of the Seine, it would be incorrect to say that the British revolt must have been confined to, or centred on, the southwest of the island. But it would certainly follow that the revolt took place in southern Britain, perhaps even including southeastern Britain. At all events, the Armoricans and other Gauls declared their independence of Rome just as the Britons had done, expelled the Imperial officials, and abolished the use of Roman law. (Those students of the period who hold the untenable view that the British revolt was directed against Constantine but not Honorius never tell us in whose favour the Armoricans rosé!) Indeed, it is extraordinary to observe

---

[38] For army-deserters in Britain during the great upset of 367/8, see Ammianus Marcellinus, *History*, XXVII.8,10, 'edictis propositis impunitateque promissa desertores ad procinctum uocabat', viz the *comes* Theodosius, father of Theodosius I.

[39] Mommsen, *Chronica Minora*, I.662; Salvian, *De Gubernatione Dei*, V.21 & 23.

[40] Rivet, *The Roman Villa*, p. 215.

[41] Frend, 'The christianization', p. 45.

[42] Borius, *Constance*, p. 93, is mistaken in saying that the Armorican revolt was one of the consequences of the great invasion of Gaul by the Vandals, Alans, and Sueves in 406. There is no suggestion in our sources that the two were in any way connected. Nor is there the slightest reason to follow Nora Chadwick, *Poetry and Letters*, p. 264f., in supposing that 'unrest in Armorica was due in a large measure to the activities of Saxon pirates along their shores'. There is no evidence for Saxon activity along the Gallic coast until we hear from Sidonius, *Carmina*, VII.369f. (cf. 390), that Saxon raids were expected on the Armorican coast in 456.

[43] See p. 71 below.

how reluctant scholars have been to accept what Zosimus clearly tells us.[44] The fact is that we have further information about the Armorican side of the revolt, which was suppressed in 417. The first way of attacking the natural interpretation of the evidence, then, is to assert that the Armorican revolt which broke out in 409 is not the same revolt as that which was crushed in 417: hence the evidence relating to 417 throws no light on what had happened in 409 – 'there is no proof of continuity', we are gravely and fatuously told.[45] Now, observe what this thesis entails. It entails believing that the Armorican revolt which broke out in 409 was put down at an unknown date. But another revolt of a different kind, though organised by those same Armoricans, thereupon broke out, and it was this second Armorican revolt which was suppressed by Exuperantius in 417. Thus, we hear of the beginning of one revolt and of the end of another! And the assumption is that we know nothing of the end of the first or of the beginning of the second! We rarely encounter this kind of gentle humour in Late Roman studies, and it is unfortunate that, when we do meet it, we must put it aside. A more economical hypothesis must be preferred to a less economical one. A single revolt involves no flight of fancy, no exercise of the inventive powers, no sense of the comical in history: a double Armorican revolt requires a good measure of all three. What the proponents of such theories never tell us[46] is in what year before 417 the Western government was in a position to undertake a campaign in the far northwest of Gaul. When was the alleged first revolt of Armorica put down? In fact, there was no year in which such a campaign could have been carried through. That is to say, the revolt was continuous from 409 to 417. It looks as though there *is* proof of continuity after all!

A second way of avoiding the obvious is to suppose that Britain and Armorica did indeed secede in 409, but that at some date after that year, though before 417, events in Armorica took a turn for the worse; the landowners' estates were taken over by the peasantry; but this was a turn which the property-respecting Britons were happily able to avoid. We cannot assume (so the argument runs) that the rebels were of the same social class in the two countries, although they had indeed been so before this later and lamentable development took place in Armorica (and only in Armorica). This development was due to the rise to power in Armorica of dastardly fellows – slaves and others – who confiscated the large estates and reduced the estate-owners to the status of slaves to their own slaves, a condition from which Exuperantius rescued them in 417. No such outrage was perpetrated in Britain.

Once more, a new chapter of history has been invented out of thin air. The movements of secession in 409 are said by Zosimus – indeed, are said emphatically by Zosimus – to have been identical. To deny that they were so

---

[44] See, for example, Stein, *Histoire*, I.252; Jones, *The Later Roman Empire*, I.191.
[45] This objection was first raised, I think, by Stevens, 'Marcus, Gratian', p. 340.
[46] Though invited to do so by Thompson, 'Britain', p. 311.

and to assert that they were different in kind or that they later on diverged and became different is to write fiction, not history.

In 410 Honorius wrote his famous letters to the city-states (the *poleis*) of Britain bidding them see to their own defence.[47] The inference is that after the revolt of 409 the unity of the British diocese and of the British provinces was shattered. Power did not fall into the hands of any diocesan or provincial councils which may or may not have existed. It was inevitable that the provinces, and *a fortiori* the diocese, should disappear as soon as the officials of the central government were expelled, for the provinces were purely administrative units which had been imposed upon Britain by the central authority and had no basis in sentiment or in anything else except the central authority's administrative convenience. It is no surprise, then, as we have seen,[48] that in 429 we hear nothing of the four or five provinces into which the British diocese had been subdivided in Roman times. Accordingly, if Honorius wanted to write to Britain at all, he was obliged to write to the *ciuitates*, for these were the largest units still existing in 410. Presumably each of them now governed itself – at any rate, for the time being – and Honorius evidently thought that each was capable of taking military action on its own account. Whether the *ciuitates* had any means of taking concerted military action Honorius's letters do not make clear. In 429 we seem to catch a glimpse (though a very indistinct one) of one *ciuitas*, or perhaps even one city, taking military action on its own initiative in an emergency against the invading Picts and Saxons.

We know from Gildas and Procopius that as the fifth century progressed the republican city-states to which Honorius had written were transformed into tyrannies or monarchies – presumably at different times in different *ciuitates*; but we have no information to let us see how the change was brought about or in what circumstances. In Gildas's day Britain (in so far as the Saxons had not occupied it) was ruled by a considerable number of kings, five of whom Gildas berates mercilessly and at least three of whom were not first-generation kings. Their kingdoms seem to bear no relation to the old *ciuitates*. The city-states as well as the provinces broke up into different fragments in the century following Germanus's visits.

That (in my view) is the historical background to the situation in Britain as Constantius describes it. It is impossible to link up in any detail the events of 409 with what we learn from Constantius of conditions in 429: not one syllable has survived in any of our sources to tell us about British affairs in the years 411–28.[49] For example, we do not know which part or parts of Britain – other than 'the South' – were affected by the revolt and secession of 409. The region of Britain which Germanus momentarily visited may or may not have been one such part. Some areas may have been more rigorously affected than others. Certainly, rich men still survived with their riches in the place where

[47] Zosimus, *History*, VI.10,2.
[48] See p. 9 above.
[49] Thompson, 'Zosimus', pp. 459–61.

Germanus debated with his opponents. But the important conclusion for our purposes is that the rebellion of 409, and the government which followed it in the relevant locality, was (according to the theory adopted here) one of peasants, *coloni*, slaves, and the like, that is to say, men who were Celtic-speaking and probably pagan. Hence, the thought that the government of the region which the saint visited in 429 may have been a government of pagans who were wholly indifferent to the sectarian squabbles of the christians will not fill us with surprise or amazement. And if the members of this pagan government did not rush down to the coast to welcome two christian bishops paying an unofficial visit from Gaul, we shall not feel astounded. And if those who organised the visits did not trouble to inform the authorities beforehand that two such visitors were expected, we shall not be open-mouthed with astonishment or stupefaction. And if none of the government's representatives sat through the debates between the Catholics and the heretics, debates which to them would have been not only tedious but downright incomprehensible, the points at issue being far beyond their understanding and also expressed in a foreign language which they did not necessarily speak or understand – if all this should turn out to be the case –, we shall not declare that we are utterly dumbfounded. And if such a government was not excessively disturbed when it noticed – if it did notice – that rich and well dressed christians were dragged off by Germanus willy-nilly to the interior of Gaul or Italy, the thought will leave us less than flabbergasted.

The hypothesis that such a government (that is, a government of poor, Celtic-speaking, rustics) seized power in 409 is based on what we are told by our one and only source of information for British history in that year, that is, on the text of Zosimus. This hypothesis is the only one which can legitimately be inferred from his words and from the relevant passage of Rutilius Namatianus.[50] What Germanus found in Britain in 429 and on his later visit is better accounted for by this than by any other theory. Any other theory? On this subject other theories are few and far between.

---

[50] Rutilius Namatianus, *De Reditu Suo*, I.213–16.

V

THE BATTLE AGAINST THE PICTS AND SAXONS

We may well call Constantius's account of the first visit to Britain cloudy and indistinct, but it must be admitted that one episode in the narrative of this visit (though not more than one) does succeed in coming to what might be called in some limited sense 'life'. This is the episode of the clash between the Britons, aided by the saint, and the Pictish and Saxon marauders. Here alone we seem to find some authentic detail, some small flash of liveliness, a shaft of pale lamplight penetrating the darkness, as though an eye-witness's account were being told at fourth or fifth hand. Indeed, the skill of Constantius in this episode is such that Nora Chadwick goes so far as to say that 'the admirable narrative style of Constantius still today succeeds in imposing this fantastic story on our sober historians'. (On this criterion I count myself a sober historian, for of all the passages in the *Vita* which relate to Britain this is the one which to my mind most carries conviction.) But it is not as convincing as many of those which narrate Germanus's actions on the Continent – for example, it can hardly compare with the description of Germanus's clash with the Alan king, Goar.[1]

The Britons of 429 are universally taunted by modern historians with their failure to handle this barbarian inroad with any military capacity. They were helpless by themselves, we are told, and could only be rescued because a Gaul – and a mere bishop at that – told them what to do. A leading scholar speaks of their 'ramshackle army' and of their 'helpless incompetence'.[2] But if we read the relevant words of Constantius with care we shall not come to that sort of conclusion.

The raid had begun when the visitors from Gaul were far away, in the place where Germanus had hurt his foot and where a fire had threatened his life (§ 16). Without any reference to the saint, the Britons had marched out to meet the enemy and were in camp; and they now sent out some very efficient scouts to reconnoitre and report (§ 17). It is nonsense to say that the Britons were 'too craven' to take the field without the encouragement of the Gallic bishops or that Germanus 'organised' their army or 'had to take the lead' or

---

[1] Chadwick, *Poetry and Letters*, p. 254; cf. Borius, *Constance*, p. 22f.
[2] Some remarks of my own in 'Britain', p. 318, are not innocent of such language.

that 'the natives had been forced to retreat'.[3] The natives had concentrated their forces to meet the raiders a considerable time before Germanus even heard of the raid and probably some days before he appeared on the scene in person. From their camp the Britons asked the help of the visiting bishops because they thought that their numbers were unequal to the coming struggle. They reached this conclusion about their numbers 'with some alarm', *trepidi*,[4] 'being apprehensive', rather than 'panic-stricken', as some would render it.[5] The bishops, who had now set out from the place where the fire had threatened Germanus, *itineris laborem subiret*,[6] promised to come, and they put on speed so as to reach the scene of the action.[7] They had evidently been a considerable distance away when the appeal reached them – perhaps two or three days' travel; and several more days elapsed before the Hallelujah battle was fought, for the bishops, when they reached the British camp, preached 'daily' to the troops, *cotidianis praedicationibus instituti*,[8] before the ambush was laid which resulted in the flight of the invaders. It may well be that a week or more elapsed between the time when the Britons notified the two bishops of the forthcoming struggle and the time when the Hallelujah battle was fought.

Up to this time, when the bishops had not reached the army, the Britons do not seem to be open to much criticism. They were now ready to make a fight of it – and there is no reason to doubt that they would have done so even if the Gallic bishops had still been at home in Gaul. It was only when the holy men had reached the camp and were raising the Britons' morale that the barbarians learned that the enemy were in camp; and they decided to surprise them 'while practically unarmed'.[9] (We must remember that the Saxons were noted for rushing forward without adequate reconnaissance.[10]) If it is necessary to use sarcasm when describing this campaign – and it appears to be the accepted practice – it would be more proper to direct it at the invaders than at the Britons. The Saxons and Picts decided to 'surprise' the Britons the best part of a week after the Britons had located them and were prepared to withstand their assault! It cannot be denied, however, that during these days of waiting the Britons made no attempt to intercept the invaders. They apparently remained inactive in their original camp –

---

[3] This last mistaken statement may be due to Hoare's translation of *quos [Britannos] eadem necessitas in castra contraxerat*, as 'the latter had been compelled to withdraw their forces within their camp'. But *contraho* here does not imply withdrawal: it means 'assemble', 'muster', 'concentrate'. Borius, *Constance*, p. 155, rightly renders, 'qu'une commune necessité avait rassemblés en un seul camp'. Groups of Britons from different places, or at any rate various groups of Britons, had joined forces in one camp.

[4] *Vita*, §17 (263,19).

[5] See, for example, Alcock, *Arthur's Britain*, p. 102, and Johnson, *Later Roman Britain*, p. 116.

[6] *Vita*, §16 (263,17).

[7] *Ibid*., §17 (264,2).

[8] *Ibid*. (264,5).

[9] *Ibid*. (264,12).

[10] So Ammianus Marcellinus, *History*, XXX.7,8, 'Saxones semper quolibet inexplorato ruentes'.

although, to be sure, they may still have been assembling their forces, and there may have been no terrain suitable for a surprise attack where the barbarians were then located: we have insufficient knowledge to frame adequate criticisms of the defence. At all events, the raiders' plans were aimed at catching the Britons unexpectedly, *quasi de inermi exercitu*,[11] and they were confident that they would be able to do so.[12] But their plan failed. The British scouts had long since detected their approach.

It was only now that Germanus announced, uninvited, that he was the Britons' leader. He picked out the British light-armed – the rest of the levy seems never to have gone into action – and led them over the intervening countryside to a place of ambush, a valley surrounded by steep sides, where he knew that he would fall in with the enemy.[13] It is true that Constantius says that Germanus 'hurried over the surrounding district', *circumiecta percurrit*,[14] but there was a limit to the amount of time at his disposal. He had already used up several days with his 'daily preachings' and can hardly have had more than a few hours at his disposal at this stage of the events. The clear implication, in my opinion, is that the enemy's route had been reported to him by the British scouts, and unless the geography of the district had been divinely revealed to him – and even Constantius does not claim that it had – the decision where to lay the ambush must have been suggested to him by the Britons, or at any rate the Britons must have placed before him the possible sites for an ambush, leaving the final decision to him (assuming, of course, that he had anything at all to do with the matter and that Constantius has not given him a prominence which he did little or nothing to deserve). After a quick look at the possibilities he was able to lay the ambush while the barbarians were still unaware that their line of march had long since been discovered and was no longer secret.[15]

In fact, what the entire incident shows more clearly than anything else is the decisive superiority of the British reconnaissance over that of the Saxons and Picts, so decisive indeed that when the Britons sprang out of their hiding-places – whether or not they yelled out the word 'Hallelujah' as they did so – the raiders panicked, threw away their arms, and took to their heels. We must not speak of the Britons 'as they closed with the enemy'. There was no hand-to-hand grapple. The Saxons and Picts panicked and fled without a struggle. Nor must we speak as though Constantius was reporting what he considered to be 'une victoire miraculeuse'. On the contrary, as Nora Chadwick wrote, 'it is remarkable that Constantius . . . should abstain from

---

[11] *Vita*, §17 (264,12).
[12] *Ibid.*, §18 (264,21).
[13] Constantius's words are, §17 (264,17), 'quo in loco nouum conponit exercitum ipse dux agminis'. Borius, *Constance*, p. 157, renders 'c'est là qu'il dispose une seconde armée', which seems wrong. Does the phrase *elegit expeditos*, §17 (264,15), imply that the Britons also had heavily armed men?
[14] *Vita*, §17 (264,15).
[15] *Ibid.*, §18 (264,20).

41

ascribing the victory to divine or miraculous agency'.[16] He does not conceal that what frightened the enemy was *not* the word 'Hallelujah' and its magic properties or even the sudden appearance of the Britons themselves, but the much more prosaic belief that an avalanche had begun and that the sky was falling![17] How Constantius or his informants could have found out the subjective feelings and motives of the raiders at this moment of crisis and panic is (to say the least) not very clear, for there is no hint that the Britons took a single prisoner.

Let us agree, then, that the Britons were by no means as spiritless and as helpless as some recent historians would have us believe. Although strategically they were on the defensive, tactically they took the initiative and went on the offensive: in the end it was they who set about attacking the invaders, and I see no reason to doubt that they would have done the same even if Germanus had never left Auxerre. The idea of the ambush, though certainly not its site (as far as I can see), may have been due to Germanus, although that in the circumstances is far from certain; and, although Constantius describes the incident so as to glorify Germanus, it is noteworthy that he makes no criticism of the Britons. Yet there is a point on which it might not be unfair to bring a criticism against the Britons. Even in his eulogy of Germanus, Constantius does not say that there was any massacre or any pursuit of the routed Saxons and Picts (to say nothing of the fact that none of them is reported to have been taken prisoner). J. Evans, therefore, well asks, 'What kind of victory was this which dispersed a large band of savages over a peaceful countryside to burn, loot, and murder as they pleased?'[18] Constantius knows nothing of the further fortunes of the defeated invaders and has no interest in them. He does not claim that Germanus obliged them to flee helter-skelter back across the Ocean to their homelands; and it may well be that they recovered from their panic in due course and turned their attention to some other luckless Britons. But although we might be tempted to criticise the Britons for failing to pursue the panic-stricken invaders, we know too little about the circumstances (for example, numbers, terrain, food-supply) to press the point.

We must not exaggerate the size and importance of the struggle. A major difficulty faced by all the northern invaders of the Imperial provinces was that of feeding themselves.[19] The raiders tended, therefore, as soon as they entered the provinces, to break up into a number of small parties which could feed themselves more easily than one large host. We do not know whether the Saxons and Picts on this occasion were part of a larger army. Assuming (as I think we ought to) that they were raiders from overseas, there may have been only a boatload or two of each of them – perhaps no more than, say, a couple of hundred men in all. Neither Prosper, who speaks of Germanus's first voyage to

---

[16] Lot, 'Bretons', p. 334; Chadwick, *Poetry and Letters*, p. 257.
[17] *Vita*, § 18 (264,23f.).
[18] Evans, 'St Germanus', p. 180.
[19] The matter is discussed by Thompson, *The Early Germans*, pp. 140–9.

Britain, nor the 'Chronicler of A.D. 452', nor anybody else except Constantius, mentions the raid. Now, the size of the foraging parties depended on a number of factors such as the fertility of the region being plundered and also the season of the year in which the raid was carried out – after the harvest had been gathered in, the foraging parties might be larger than in winter. If a couple of hundred warriors were in the plundering band on this occasion, they would soon have been obliged to split up into smaller parties unless they had been lucky enough to find – and to find without delay – a villa with well stocked barns or a prosperous and unfortified village. But well stocked barns will have been few and far between at this time of year; for we must remember that the incident took place at Easter-time. By that date last year's grain will have been largely consumed, whereas the harvest of 429 will not have been long in the ground. Indeed, we may suspect that Saxon and Pict alike would have been lucky enough if they had been able to bring with them from home sufficient food to last them for more than a very few days after setting foot in southern Britain.

The raiders hoped to catch the Britons unarmed, although they knew that they were in the field. We must not take this to mean that the Saxons and Picts hoped to surprise the Britons by attacking a district which they had not attacked before, a district which, never having been attacked, might regard itself therefore as immune from attack. The raiders planned to take them by surprise due to the speed of their approach.[20] On the other hand, de Plinval may go too far when he speaks of 'le raid saisonnier des Saxons'.[21] I do not know whether that is the right phrase to use, but certainly there is no reason to think that this was the first raid on this district of Britain. The Saxons knew enough about the Britons in this neighbourhood to feel sure that if they hurried they might be able to fall upon them before they had time to arm themselves. That seems to imply that they more or less knew what to expect, that they had had some experience of them on previous occasions. On the other hand, they may not have been wholly familiar with the terrain where they planned to attack the Britons, for they found themselves on the wrong side of the river in which some of them were eventually drowned,[22] and had to cross it when advancing on the Britons and re-cross it when fleeing before them. The Britons, too, knew what to do when the crisis came: they went out and encamped in an appropriate place and sent out their very efficient scouts. They were only dismayed by the reports, presumably brought back by the scouts, that they were considerably outnumbered by the intruders. What the incident shows clearly enough is that the Britons of this area and these Picts and Saxons – though not *all* Picts and Saxons – were already familiar with each other's methods of warfare. This was by no means the first time that the Britons of this neighbourhood had seen a barbarian raider. According to the

[20] *Vita*, § 17 (264,12).
[21] De Plinval, 'Les campagnes', p. 146.
[22] *Vita*, § 18 (265,3).

Gallic 'Chronicle of A.D. 452',[23] Britain had suffered various 'disasters and adversities' before the year 446/7 and in that year 'fell under the dominion of the Saxons'. Whatever the meaning of that last phrase, it is clear that the 'various disasters and adversities' extended back to 429 and even earlier, for, as we have seen, raids appear to have been a familiar enough phenomenon by that year, although (no doubt) conditions in the 430s became very much worse. Also, the complete absence from all our authorities of reference to Saxon raids on the coasts of Gaul in the early years of the fifth century has a sinister meaning for the Britons:[24] with Britain so close at hand, there was no need for the raiders to go farther afield and harry Armorica or the western seaboard of Gaul.

The working agreement between the Saxons and the Picts is remarkable. It is the only instance of such cooperation to have been recorded from the age of the migrations. It is true that in 367 the so-called 'barbarian conspiracy', *barbarica conspiratio*, mentioned by Ammianus Marcellinus,[25] entailed simultaneous attacks on the Roman provinces by peoples whom that historian[26] calls Dicalydones and Uerturiones (both of them branches of the Picts), the *Scotti* from Ireland, the *Attacotti* from Heaven-knows-where, and on the Continent the Franks and Saxons. The first four of these attacked Britain, but the Franks and Saxons invaded Gaul by land and sea – the former by land, the latter by sea[27] – so that in 367 there was no cooperation in the field between Saxon and Pict, no fighting shoulder to shoulder as they did, or intended to do, in 429. In all probability the *conspiratio* of 367 was due to nothing more than coincidence. Perhaps the Picts and Irish decided to attack simultaneously, perhaps the Franks and Saxons did so; but more probably, I think, all these peoples saw their opportunity at the one time when the Emperor was newly come to the throne. Certainly, it is hard to believe that the 'conspiracy' was organised by one man, a barbarian of unusual diplomatic skill and persuasiveness – and an above-average linguist into the bargain – who rushed from Ireland to Pictland and from Pictland to Germany and back again, to and fro, arranging a joint attack on the Empire by all and sundry at one and the same time!

[23] §126: ed. Mommsen, *Chronica Minora*, II.660.
[24] No Saxon raids on the Gallic coasts are known until 456: see p. 35, n. 42, above.
[25] Ammianus Marcellinus, *History*, XXVII.8,1.
[26] *Ibid.*, XXVII.8,5.
[27] So I interpret the passage of Ammianus cited in the previous note: 'gallicanos uero tractus Franci et Saxones, eisdem confines, quo quisque erumpere potuit, terra uel mari, praedis acerbis incendiisque, et captiuorum funeribus omnium uiolabant'. But Ammianus, XXVI.4,5, contradicts his own statement when he summarises the invasions carried out at the beginning of the joint reign of Valentinian and Valens: 'Picti Saxonesque et Scotti et Attacotti Britannos aerumnis uexauere continuis'. It is safer to follow the detailed narrative in XXVII.8,5 than this brief summary, from which he has accidentally omitted the Franks. And that this course is correct is confirmed by Ammianus's third reference to the event: in XXX.7,8f., he writes his 'obituary' of Valentinian I and clearly distinguishes the Saxon raid from events in Britain. On the events of 367–8 see further p. 52, n. 38, below. Ammianus is (second to Tacitus) the greatest of the extant Latin historians. (I say 'Latin' rather than 'Roman' as he was in fact a Greek of Antioch.) The best introduction to his work is that of Blockley, *Ammianus*.

44

Gildas stresses that the normal practice of the Picts was to attack Britain by sea.[28] Presumably, then, in 429 two parties of sea-raiders, one Saxon, one Pictish, encountered one another and agreed to cooperate for the time being. It does not follow, however, that in the previous winter messages flew across the North Sea from Pictland to Germany and back again from Germany to Pictland. The two parties presumably fell in with one another when they were already off the British coast, and agreed to join forces for the time being in plundering the Britons. The fact of their agreeing to cooperate suggests that each band was small: cooperation would thus be easier to arrange and carry into effect than if the two companies had been large, jealous of their prestige, under a plurality of leaders, and all alike equally hungry, hungry for fame as well as for food. Incidentally, it would be interesting to know in what language they negotiated their agreement. Hodgkin quotes the view that 'the alliance between Pictish-speaking Highlanders and German-speaking Saxons seems so great an improbability that it is reasonable to see in it one of the author's imaginative touches intended to enhance the fame of the saint, a victory over two peoples being more miraculous than a victory over one'.[29] Hodgkin himself rejects this view – and rightly, for although Constantius may have invented or exaggerated this and that so as to glorify his hero, this *sort* of invention – an alliance between Picts and Saxons – is not at all what a late fifth-century hagiographer would have devised.

The incident which culminated in the Hallelujah battle shows clearly that the aim of the united invaders at the moment when Constantius gives us a glimpse of them was to bring the Britons to battle and to defeat them in the field. But what then? If they had won their victory, did they aim to settle in that part of Britain? The fact that there is no reference in Constantius's narrative to the invaders' women and children means nothing. If the raiders had been accompanied by their womenfolk and their children they would presumably have left them under guard at the ships while they tried to wipe out the menfolk of the district.

The aim of the raiders was presumably to acquire fame among their countrymen and loot from the Britons. They would doubtless take food, wine, weapons, luxury goods of all kinds, cattle, though whether (like the Pictish raiders of 367) they would also take prisoners, other than women, depends on the Saxons' need for slave-labour.[30] The Picts of 367 undoubtedly took prisoners other than women.[31] They would certainly not take prisoners in order to hold them to ransom: it would be impossible for a Briton to ransom a

[28] Gildas, *De Excidio*, I.XIV, XVI, XVII. I do not know whether cavalry was known in Caledonia at this date – it certainly was later on – but since the Picts arrived in Britain by sea (as I am convinced) they fought as infantry, not as cavalry: hence *Panegyrici Latini*, XII (II).5,2. 'attritam pedestribus proeliis Britanniam referam? Saxo consumptus bellis naualibus offeretur.' The first of these questions must refer to the Picts (or to the Picts and Irish), the Saxons being dealt with in the second.
[29] Hodgkin, *A History*, I.61.
[30] See p. 95 below.
[31] Ammianus Marcellinus, *History*, XXVII.8,7, discussed on p. 52, n. 38, below.

relative who had been carried off to the Highlands or to the Continent, just as it was impossible for his relatives to ransom St Patrick from Co. Mayo. There was no way of knowing even to the nearest hundred miles where the unfortunate prisoner had been carried to.

It seems a long and dangerous journey to undertake merely in order to win such booty as might, or might not, come to hand from a small tract of the sub-Roman British countryside. But of course the risks that the raiders ran were small by comparison with those braved by seven shiploads of Heruls (from Denmark?) who appeared off the north coast of Spain in 455 and cruelly plundered some districts there, and then made their way home.[32] In fact, we know nothing of the motives or the state of mind of the Saxons (to say nothing of the Picts) on the eve of the migrations. Was the idea of migrating to the former Roman province already in the air in the Saxon homeland as early as 429? Were they already collecting not only loot and fame but also geographical knowledge of the region where they would one day live? Were they testing out the valour of the inhabitants? What would bring into being the idea of a mass-migration? It would presumably come into being gradually as the raids were found to be more and more often successful, as the land of the province was found to be uniformly more fertile than their own fields at home and the inhabitants easy enough to defeat (in spite of a local setback in 429). At any rate, that is approximately what Anglo-Saxons of a much later date thought to have happened: early immigrants sent back word of 'the worthlessness of the Britons and of the excellence of the land'.[33]

We have argued that the raid of 429 which Germanus helped to defeat may have been carried out by no more than a couple of hundred barbarians; and, if that was indeed the case, it would follow that the Britons – since there is no reason to doubt that their scouts' report was false or alarmist – will not have been numbered in thousands. This was a small-scale action, and R. H. Hodgkin was probably right to call it a 'skirmish'.[34] No doubt the news of it reached the ears of the man of tribunician power; but few will think that Aetius ever heard of it or that it kept Valentinian III from his sleep.

[32] Hydatius, *Chronicle*, §171 (ed. Mommsen, *Chronica Minora*, II.28). I wonder how the Spaniards knew that these pirates were Heruls rather than Saxons or Franks.
[33] *Anglo-Saxon Chronicle*, *s.a.* 449E, in Whitelock, *English Historical Documents*, pp. 153–4 (cf. p. 113 on this version).
[34] Hodgkin, *A History*, I.61.

VI

GEOGRAPHY REAL AND IMAGINARY

It is as certain as anything can be in the biography of St Germanus that both his visits to Britain took him to one and the same place in the island. Some time ago, when I thought that his second visit took place after the calamity in the 440s reported by the Gallic 'Chronicle of A.D. 452', I suggested that the second visit might have brought Germanus and his companion, Severus, to a more westerly part of the island than that which he had reached in 429.[1] The idea was not an original one: I had forgotten that it had already been put forward by Paul Grosjean, who was followed by Borius in his edition of Constantius's *Vita*. That suggestion should be rejected.[2]

Let us examine the language in which Constantius describes the arrival of Germanus and Severus in Britain on the second visit. Rumours kept spreading the news[3] in Britain that Germanus was on the way.[4] Elafius heard these rumours, presumably while the bishops were still at sea, and hurried to meet them with all the 'province' following him. The bishops arrived, the ignorant multitude met them,[5] the bishops blessed them and poured out the teaching of the divine word. The text then goes on to tell us that Germanus 'recognised that the people were holding out in that state of belief in which he had left them', *recognoscit populum in ea qua reliquerat credulitate durantem*, only a handful being adherents of Pelagius.[6] The saint then turned to deal with Elafius's lame son. All this – the blessing of the crowd, the preaching of a sermon, and the cure of Elafius's son – took place at the spot where they all

---

[1] See p. 55 below.

[2] Thompson, 'Gildas', p. 215; Grosjean, 'Notes', p. 177; Borius, *Constance*, p. 84. The view that Germanus did not journey to the west on the second visit is rightly maintained by Evans, 'St Germanus', p. 185. Doubt has been thrown on the chronology of the Gallic 'Chronicle of A.D. 452', at any rate as Mommsen presents it: see Miller, 'The last British entry'; cf. Casey, 'Magnus Maximus'. It is clear now that the matter urgently requires further study. Cf. p. 92 below.

[3] *Vita*, § 26 (270,2), *nuntiabant*, imperfect.

[4] Note *uenire, ibid.* (270,1), not *uenisse*, which would mean that the rumour spread that he had already arrived.

[5] I do not know why the multitude is described as *inscia*. Constantius says that for the most part the people had preserved their orthodoxy: in what way, then, does he consider them to be *inscia*? Hoare, *The Western Fathers*, p. 307, translates 'unexpectedly'.

[6] *Vita*, § 26 (270,8).

met.[7] What then is the meaning of 'that state of belief in which he had left them', *reliquerat?* There is no hint in this part of the story that there had been any interval when Germanus was away from this multitude or that the visitors had left the place for a while and had then come back. The words *in ea qua reliquerat credulitate* must therefore refer to 'the faith in which he had left them' when he had last been among them, and that can only mean in 429. It cannot refer to the faith in which he had left them at any earlier stage of the present (the second) visit, for during the present visit he had not left them at any time. That sentence could not have been written, I should suggest, if the inhabitants of two different areas of Britain were concerned in the two visits. Of course, as a matter of strict accuracy, this does not prove that both visits brought Germanus to the same spot, but it does prove, I think, that this was how Constantius saw the events: he knew, or he assumed, that Germanus visited the same place on both occasions. And in this connexion that is as much as we can hope to know.

The first scene described by Constantius in his account of the visit of 429 takes place on the seashore or in the port where Germanus and Lupus first set foot in Britain. After the storm which beset them in the Channel, he says, 'in a little while they were enjoying the peace and quiet of the shore for which they longed. Here a multitude coming together from different directions received the bishops', (*breui optati litoris quiete potiuntur. Ibi conueniens ex diuersis partibus multitudo excepit sacerdotes*).[8] A throng of people, then, came in from the surrounding countryside. But nothing much seems to have happened at the place where they landed apart from the welcoming of the bishops by the crowd and the expulsion of various evil spirits from those of whom they had taken possession (whatever we are to understand by that achievement). But after that, says Constantius,[9] they filled the island of Britain with their reputation, preaching, and miracles. Every day crowds thronged round them, and they preached 'not only in churches but also at crossroads, through the countryside, in out-of-the-way places . . . everywhere', *non solum in ecclesiis uerum etiam per triuia, per rura, per deuia . . . passim.*[10] The whole 'region' came over to their opinion.[11] From all this it is clear that they have now moved out of the port and are travelling through the country. But we may disregard the statement that they filled the *Britanniarum insulam*[12] with their preaching. Like the statement that the news of their arrival spread 'through the whole island',[13] this must be an overstatement designed to glorify the saint. I would certainly find it hard to follow de Plinval when he takes Germanus to the borders of Scotland and even to Candida Casa,[14]

---

[7] So Grosjean, 'Notes', p. 175.

[8] *Vita*, § 13 (260,18). Note that the words *optati litoris* here suggest that Germanus landed and was welcomed on an open beach, not in a port; but I doubt if we should press the point.

[9] *Ibid.*, § 14 (260,25).

[10] *Ibid.* (261,2).

[11] *Ibid.* (261,6).

[12] *Ibid.* (260,24).

[13] *Ibid.*, § 26 (270,1).

[14] De Plinval, 'Les campagnes', p. 146.

although other scholars have not hesitated to take him to north Wales. Indeed, there is no necessary reason to think that the Pelagian heresy had reached to every part of Britain: it is wholly unknown to Gildas, so that we may think that it never came to his part of the island.[15] On the other hand, these phrases undoubtedly imply that the two bishops did not stay in the port or on the beach where they had landed. The scene of the events is undefined except that they were now on their way to the place where a little later they were to debate with the Pelagians. At this stage of the bishops' travels the Pelagians lay low and did not come out to counter them.[16]

True to his practice when telling of British affairs, Constantius gives no location for the scene of the great debate with the Pelagians and of the miraculous healing of the blind daughter of the man of tribunician power. It is hard to forgive him for this gross omission, whatever the purpose of his book may have been. But the language of the *Vita*[17] shows (beyond any reasonable doubt, in my opinion) that the debate with the heretics did *not* take place in Verulamium.[18] If the debate had taken place there, the bishops would have behaved in an exceedingly offhand and indeed disrespectful manner to St Alban: they waited until the debate and its antecedents were over and the blind girl healed before they took the trouble to pay a visit to the martyr's shrine. And although the word *petierunt*[19] does not necessarily imply a considerable journey, it equally does not suggest that they were already in Verulamium and now did nothing more than amble a few hundred yards along the road to visit the shrine of St Alban at last as an afterthought, all other business having been brought to a satisfactory conclusion. Indeed, if they did no more than that, Constantius might not have considered it worth recording the visit to the shrine at all, at any rate in the form in which he does record it. It seems to me most likely that after the miracle of the tribune's daughter the two bishops set out on a relatively long journey rather than that they were already in Verulamium and now took an afternoon's stroll to pay their belated respects to the martyr.[20] We can be reasonably sure, then, that the bishops paid a visit to three places in Britain – the port or beach where they landed, the place where the organisers of the visit had arranged for the debate with the Pelagians to take place, and Verulamium – and, of course, the intervening roads. Beyond that statement we cannot safely go.

But since Constantius has told us so much in general and so little in

[15] See p. 22 above.
[16] *Vita*, § 14 (261,7).
[17] *Ibid*., § 16 (262,13f.).
[18] So, rightly, Alcock, *Arthur's Britain*, p. 188. Lot, 'Bretons', p. 334, goes so far as to speak of 'un concile tenu à Verulam'. On Verulamium in the fifth century see Wacher, *The Towns*, pp. 220–5, with references.
[19] *Vita*, § 16 (262,14).
[20] Levison, 'St Alban', p. 344, says that the *martyrium* of St Alban 'can be ascribed to Verulamium and St Alban's, as far as certainty or probability is at all applicable to such traditions'. Note the doubt of Borius, *Constance*, p. 86; but scepticism in this matter could be overdone.

particular about Germanus's first visit to Britain, it is tempting to throw discretion to the winds and to inject into his story a geographical framework, even though this cannot be supported by any superfluity of evidence. Such a flight of fancy can show us the *kind* of thing which may have been involved in the visit of 429. I should put forward a conjectural route for the saint which (i) appears to account for all the evidence, (ii) contradicts none of it, and (iii) is in itself not improbable. I suggest that few other hypotheses will explain so much while leaving the evidence uncontradicted, although this may be an optimistic view. But I cannot stress sufficiently that this hypothesis is suggested here simply and solely *exempli gratia*. It is make-believe.

The pope and the Gallic bishops would have had little reason for concern if the news had reached them that Pelagianism had won over a country town like Winchester[21] or Chichester or Dorchester or some similar Romano–British 'Hicksville'. On the other hand, the pope and the Gallic bishops would have had excellent reason for alarm if news had reached them that Pelagianism had won over to its cause the inhabitants of London or a great part of them. London, we need not doubt, was still by far the largest centre of population in Britain. The road-system of the entire island was based on it, so that the heresy, once successful in London, could 'vomit its poison' – I borrow this elegant metaphor from Gildas[22] – over the rest of the island with no trouble as far as communications were concerned. Worse still – far worse –, the heretics could easily disgorge their poison through the southeastern ports back into Gaul from which their doctrines had been expelled with such effort on the part of Church and State alike only a few years earlier. R. H. Hodgkin rightly said that 'the fire of heresy had to be extinguished in Britain lest it spread to the Continent'.[23] Let us suppose, then, that the debate with the Pelagians was held in London and that the heretics' successes among the inhabitants of London had been very extensive, *in populo quem subuerterant*.[24] The visitors went to St Albans. Now, from London the distance to Verulamium is only twenty-two miles (twenty-one, according to the Antonine Itinerary).[25] So a day's easy tramp would take the bishops from the one place to the other when the debate was over. (On the Continent Germanus seems to have travelled by horse; and if he did so in Britain, the length of the journey to Verulamium would be negligible. But in fact on the Continent Germanus, when he travelled on horseback, travelled only by the horses of the public

---

[21] Borius, *Constance*, p. 84 (cf. the map on his p. 212), is inclined to bring the visitors to the Solent and thence to Winchester.
[22] *De Excidio*, 12,3.
[23] Hodgkin, *A History*, I.72.
[24] *Vita*, §14 (261,10).
[25] On this matter see Rivet & Smith, *The Place-names*, pp. 157–60, 164–6. Other students of the period who seem to have toyed with London as the scene of the debate are Lot, 'Bretons', p. 334f.; Hodgkin, *A History*, I.61, who suggests that Pictish sea-raiders coming down the east coast 'might well cause fear among the militia of London and of Verulam', but he is inclined to place the Hallelujah battle 'in the hills of the Chiltern escarpment'. So, too, Alcock, *Arthur's Britain*, p. 102.

post; and since the public post is unlikely to have been functioning still in Britain – it had been organised by the Praetorian Prefect and the provincial governors, not by the *ciuitates* – we had best suppose that he travelled on foot.) From Winchester or Chichester or Cirencester or the like, then, the bishops would have wasted several days on the road to and from Verulamium, and would have done so to no purpose whatever, for on this journey they are not said to have preached to the heretics or to the wavering Catholics, still less to the pagans.

At an early stage of the return journey from St Alban's shrine to the port of embarkation the saint was nearly the victim of a fire. He had reached a built-up area where the thatched houses were constructed so close together that the fire spread rapidly from one to the other. The saint escaped by a miracle, according to Constantius, and a 'crowd beyond counting', *turba sine numero*,[26] collected. Now, Constantius often speaks of a 'crowd', *multitudo*,[27] *frequentia*,[28] and *turba*,[29] and so on, when narrating events in Britain. But on three occasions he goes out of his way to indicate a very large crowd indeed: *inmensae multitudinis numerositas*[30] and *regionis uniuersitas*,[31] both referring to the scene of the great debate, that is, according to our hypothesis, London. (If we may press *regionis uniuersitas*, we can suppose that people flocked into the place of the debate from the surrounding countryside.) The third such phrase, *turba sine numero*, indicates the crowd at the place where the fire broke out. The situation now is that Germanus is on his way back from St Alban's shrine to the port from which he would sail home to Gaul and has reached a large built-up area a considerable distance from that port. Would it be farfetched to suppose simply that we are now back again in London, that is to say, that this fire happened when the saint was in London on the return journey? What other place of note would he pass through on this part of his travels? It must be admitted, of course, that, were it not for the phrase *turba sine numero*,[32] any small town (Rochester, for example), any village perhaps, would suit the description of the place well enough. But an argument based on an author's references to 'a crowd' as against 'a big crowd' cannot carry much weight.

When the Count Theodosius and his men travelled from Gaul to Britain in 367 they sailed from Boulogne to Richborough.[33] When Constantine III set sail from Britain to Gaul in 407, he embarked at an unknown port in Britain and arrived at Boulogne.[34] Polemius Silvius writing in 449 speaks of Boulogne as the port for Britain, although the question has been raised – I do not know

[26] *Vita*, § 16 (263,11).
[27] *Ibid.*, § 13 (260,19).
[28] *Ibid.*, § 14 (261,1).
[29] *Ibid.*, § 16 (263,6 & 9).
[30] *Ibid.*, § 14 (261,12).
[31] *Ibid.* (261,6).
[32] *Ibid.*, § 16 (263,11).
[33] Ammianus Marcellinus, *History*, XXVII.8,7.
[34] Zosimus, *History*, VI.2,2.

why – whether he is referring to the time when he was writing or to a considerably earlier date.[35] Boulogne, then, would have been the likely port of departure for Germanus. (As a matter of fact, Constantius gives us a hint as to the place where he embarked but unfortunately he does so in a phrase which we cannot interpret, *de sinu gallico*.[36]) Whether the saint landed at Dover or Richborough or elsewhere there is no means of saying. But from one of these British ports, whichever it may have been, he would have made his way along the road to Canterbury and thence to London, according to the hypothesis which we are discussing. It is on this journey that he is said to have preached *non solum in ecclesiis uerum etiam per triuia, per rura, per deuia*.[37] No doubt he strayed off the road here and there where he could find an audience of Pelagians or of wavering Catholics. If we accept this as his itinerary from the coast through London to Verulamium and back again, it would follow that he was still in London, though on the point of leaving it, when he received the appeal for help against the Picts and Saxons, and hence that it was after he left London on the return journey to the coast that he fell in with the British defenders against the barbarian intruders. That would suggest some place in northern Kent as the scene of the Hallelujah victory; and it must be remembered that in 367, as Theodosius made his way along this very road from Richborough to London, he was obliged to scatter wandering bands of Pictish plunderers, loaded with booty and driving off cattle and prisoners.[38] Germanus and his men, then, were fighting on ground which was no stranger to conflicts of Romans and invaders. After the victory the bishops resumed their journey homewards, *reditum moliuntur*,[39] continuing their way presumably to Canterbury and thence to the port. Whether the river in which some of the raiders were drowned was the Medway or the Stour I leave to others to consider.

Students of place-names have drawn attention to the relatively high rate of survival of Romano-British settlement-names along the north and east coasts of Kent – from London to Richborough and from Dover to Pevensey.[40] The most likely explanation, in my view, is that the Saxons were tolerably familiar with the major ports on this coast as a result of raiding and trading

[35] Mommsen, *Chronica Minora*, I.537: 'Belgica Secunda de qua transitur ad Britanniam'. For Mommsen's changes of mind about the date of this reference see H. Dessau *apud* Mommsen, *Gesammelte Schriften*, VII.657n. But Rivet & Smith, *The Place-names*, p. 81, refer the passage to *ca* 385. I know of no convincing evidence that the Franks at this date had cut the road from Auxerre through Sens to Boulogne.

[36] *Vita*, § 13 (259,15).

[37] *Ibid.*, § 14 (261,2).

[38] Ammianus Marcellinus, *History*, XXVII.8,7, a passage where Rolfe's translation is seriously misleading. Rolfe, *Ammianus*, III.54, renders the words as though Theodosius attacked the *uastatoriae manus* only *after* he had reached London, whereas the historian is quite clear that he attacked them *tendens ad Lundinium*. The passage is taken correctly by Tomlin, 'The date', p. 306, and by Blockley, 'The date', p. 224f. On the British campaign of 367 in general, see Austin, *Ammianus*, pp. 42–6.

[39] *Vita*, § 18 (265,10).

[40] Gelling, *Signposts*, pp. 60–2, following Hogg, 'The survival'. But note Jackson, *Language and History*, p. 197.

for generations past, and so the place-names were embedded in their language before they ever dreamed of settling there permanently. It is the most exposed part of the entire island to the approach of traders and the aggression of raiders from that part of the Continent which lay outside the Roman frontier. The view that the survival of the place-names means the survival of the British inhabitants is, in my view, singularly mistaken.

What exactly, then, are the reasons for suggesting that the great debate with the Pelagians took place in London? It must be confessed that they are unimpressive, but, such as they are, they are threefold. (i) The place contained a sufficiently large population to involve a relatively dangerous number of people in the heresy – dangerous, that is to say, to the Church and to the orthodox belief; and from this centre the infection could spread out along the great roads more readily than from any other city in Britain. It could also – and this would be the essential point for the pope and the Gallic bishops – spread back to Gaul, for the experience of Germanus himself shows that communications between Britain and Gaul were still uninterrupted. Admittedly, this last matter could indicate other towns besides London. (ii) A journey to Verulamium from any other considerable city would have consumed to little purpose a disproportionate amount of the visiting bishops' time, given that they may not have had very much time at their disposal. (iii) A raid carried out by a joint force of Picts and Saxons at this date is nothing of a surprise on the exposed north coast of Kent. We have seen that Count Theodosius in 367 had to round up raiding bands of Picts, Irish, and *Attacotti* in this very area.[41]

There is no need to stress that these three considerations by no means amount to a certainty or even to a strong probability. But it is not easy to think of an hypothesis which would be less objectionable than this one. The second city of southern Britain was Cirencester. A glance at the map will show, among other things, that only superhuman Picts could have made their way into its vicinity. But on the whole if a critic were to say that Lincoln or York are just as possible as London for the scene of the debate with the Pelagians, it would not be easy to refute him;[42] and he could point to the words *Britanniarum insulam . . . apostolici sacerdotes raptim opinione, praedicatione, uirtutibus impleuerunt*[43] – 'the apostolic bishops rapidly filled the island of the Britains with their reputation, preaching, and miracles' – to support his case, a phrase which on our hypothesis we must write off as a rhetorical flourish.

[41] Ammianus Marcellinus, *History*, XXVII.8,7f., where his phrase *mersam difficultatibus summis antehac ciuitatem* presumably refers to London's military difficulties with the invaders at an earlier date. This suggests that in 429 Pictish raiders were by no means unknown in the neighbourhood of London.

[42] In fact, Evans, 'St Germanus', p. 182, thinks that 'since the encounter clearly took place somewhere in the North it is possible that soldiers provided by the two *coloniae* of York and Lincoln formed the backbone of the force' which won the Hallelujah victory. Evans does not say why he would place the battle in the North: perhaps it is because of the presence of Picts, but this does not follow, as is shown by the experiences of Count Theodosius in 367.

[43] *Vita*, § 14 (260,24).

But would the pope have cared very much about what happened at this date in Lincoln or York? Would the Gallic clergy ever have heard of events there? What went on in those two places was not likely to have much influence on Gaul or to have roused the pope from his day-to-day activities. And what reason would have taken the Pelagian missionary Agricola so far afield? If he had to take himself off to Lincoln, are we to conclude that he had failed in London and the South? But if he had proved a failure in the major cities of the South, it is improbable that anyone would have sent for the Gallic bishops to come over as a matter of urgency in order to undo his work – improbable, too, that Prosper would have considered him worth several lines in his *Chronicle*.

But if Agricola is an improbable preacher in Lincoln and York, and Picts are unlikely raiders in Winchester and Dorchester, perhaps our London theory, as it makes its debut, need not wear an altogether shamefaced, woebegone, sheepish, or hangdog look.

VII

THE DATE OF THE SECOND VISIT TO BRITAIN

In 1957 I ventured to publish a chronological note on St Germanus of Auxerre and to suggest the year 444 as the date of his second visit to Britain and 445 as the date of his death at Ravenna.[1] *Horresco referens*. No sooner had the article appeared than Paul Grosjean pointed out to me that that date was untenable: according to Constantius, Germanus reached Milan on 19 June and Ravenna at the beginning of July, and on his arrival there he met the Emperor Valentinian III.[2] But in fact he could not have done so in 445, for early in July of that year Valentinian was not in Ravenna: he was in Rome, where he published his Novel 17 on 8 July. Grosjean told me in a letter dated 23 June 1957 that, in spite of what he had himself published that same year, he had come to the conclusion that in fact the year 448 best suits the evidence relating to the death of the saint.[3]

I agreed with him at the time, but now after a quarter of a century I have come back to the study of this same problem and while writing the following pages have often thought of Paul Grosjean, a great and kindly man. He might not have accepted my conclusions (in so far as there are any conclusions in these pages) but he would certainly have welcomed any attempt to find out more about the saint of Auxerre.

That Germanus visited Britain for the first time in 429 is attested by Prosper of Aquitaine[4] and, as far as I know, this date has never been called in question. It looks as though the events of this first visit took place remarkably early in the year. Germanus and Lupus were appointed, crossed the Channel, preached, defeated the Pelagians, visited the shrine of St Alban, Germanus hurt his foot and recovered from his injury, and he led the army which would soon put the Pictish and Saxon marauders to flight – all this before Easter.[5] Since the events which occurred during the visit to Britain must have taken up a few weeks at least, we may suppose that Germanus and Lupus did not

---

[1] Thompson, 'A chronological note'.
[2] See p. 65, n. 50, below.
[3] Grosjean, 'Notes', p. 185.
[4] Prosper, § 1301 (ed. Mommsen, *Chronica Minora*, I.472).
[5] *Vita*, § 17 (264,8).

set out from Gaul later than March. That would be consistent with their crossing the Channel in a gale (although only a limited number of people believes that summer-storms are impossible in the English Channel). In fact, winter-crossings were considered to be noteworthy but were not unknown, although there is no need to assume one in this case.[6] After the victory over the barbarians the visiting bishops would hardly have spent many days in Britain; they would have returned to Gaul by mid- or late April. It was the opinion of de Plinval, however, that Germanus set out in the late summer of 429, spent some seven months in Britain, and returned home immediately after Easter in 430.[7] There is no evidence that Germanus stayed away from his see for so long but, although I have put this chronology on one side, it would not be at all easy to refute it. To be sure, it would mean that Constantius's account of the first British visit is even more inadequate than we normally think it to be. But what could Germanus achieve in as short a visit as both I and others have assumed? We should have to suppose that the chief result of his journey to Britain in 429 was a lifting of the morale of the British Catholics and a confirmation of the Britons' hope that in Gaul they were not forgotten – and, of course, a corresponding blow to the confidence of the Pelagians.

It seems to be agreed on all sides that St Germanus's second visit took place at some date in the 440s. Nearly all scholars place it in the period 444–448, although de Plinval, the distinguished historian of Pelagianism, is heterodox in this respect and places it in the first years of the papacy of Leo I – say, in 440–2.[8] As Ralph Mathisen remarks in a valuable paper on Germanus, 'Easily dated events allow Germanus' death to be placed between 444, when he was present with Hilary of Arles at the deposition of Bishop Chelidonius of Besançon, and 450, when the Empress Galla Placidia, whom Germanus met at Ravenna, died'.[9] Much has been written on the subject in recent times, and it has not been doubted, as far as I know, that the bishop

[6] For winter-crossings to Britain see Ammianus Marcellinus, *History*, XX.1,3, and Firmicus Maternus, *De errore profanarum religionum*, XXVIII.6, references which I owe to Tomlin, 'The date', p. 396, n. 25. I have disregarded the *Vita S. Lupi*, §4 (edd. Krusch & Levison, *Passiones*, VII.284–302, at p. 297), *temporibus hibernis*, for that *Vita* appears to have no independent value: see Krusch's discussion, *ibid.*, p. 284f.

[7] De Plinval, 'Les campagnes', p. 145f.

[8] *Idem*, *Pélage*, p. 382, n. 4. Similarly, Bury, *A History*, I.250, n. 2, dates the Armorican rebellion in which St Germanus became involved, together with the death of the saint, to 442, but *ibid.*, I.201, n. 2, he dates the second visit to Britain 'probably about 440', a small but most uncharacteristic inconsistency. The view of Chadwick, *Poetry and Letters*, pp. 256–60, that the second visit is unhistorical and a mere duplication of the first, has not won acceptance among recent writers. There is little relevant to our purpose in Gessel, 'Germanus'.

[9] Mathisen, 'The last year', p. 152. The same scholar's paper, 'Hilarius', is a careful discussion of the whole Celidonius-affair. In the former paper Mathisen would most ingeniously identify the *artifices* of the *Vita*, §31 (274,7), with those of Diehl, *Inscriptiones*, no. 1806, but unhappily there is no reason to think that they had connexions with Narbonne. On them see also Claude, 'Die Handwerker', pp. 223 and 244.

died on 31 July:[10] but in what year? That it was some year in the period 440–8 is nowadays one of the accepted facts of Gallic and of British history in the fifth century A.D.

I should suggest that this is not an established fact at all, and that Germanus may well have visited Britain and Ravenna in 437. I should put this opinion forward as a possibility, even a probability, and hope that others will either confirm it or bury it out of sight.

An important reason for thinking that Germanus was still alive in the 440s is to be found in a passage of the *Vita S. Hilarii Arelatensis*.[11] It seems that this work was written by an otherwise unknown Reverentius about the year 500 or perhaps in the early years of the sixth century. It is intended as a work of edification, and the author also seeks to glorify Hilary; but it has been argued that his work is of limited historical value. That may well be true of the work as a whole, but it is certainly the case that in its account of Celidonius, Hilary, and Pope Leo[12] it preserves much authentic and valuable information in spite of its bias. The author tells of the collaboration of Hilary and Germanus in the matter of Celidonius of Besançon. Hilary, we are told, often sought out Germanus, with whom he used to discuss the lives and work of his clergy. Various informers and tale-bearers (as we should call them, though the writer of the *Vita S. Hilarii* does not regard them as such) flocked to the two bishops to inform them (i) of how Celidonius had married a widow, and (ii) of how, when he had been an official of the government, he had not hesitated to inflict the death-penalty. Both these actions, they held, made Celidonius ineligible to serve as a bishop. Thereupon Hilary and Germanus ordered an enquiry to be instituted.[13] After his condemnation Celidonius went to Rome to protest against his condemnation. Hilary also went to Rome but was severely reprimanded by Leo I, in his *Epistle 10*, and the pope's position was upheld and confirmed by the Emperor Valentinian III in his *Novel 17*. This *Novel* was published on 8 July 445 and provides us with our only date for the entire incident. Scholars have therefore assumed that the whole story of the attack on Celidonius must be dated to 444/5, and hence that Germanus was alive in that year.

[10] Grosjean, 'Notes', p. 180, regards the date 31 July as certain. It is given in the *Martyrologium Hieronymianum* and in *De gestis episcoporum Autissiodorensium*, §7 (ed. Migne, *Patrologia Latina*, CXXXVIII.228); cf. [Krusch &] Levison, *Passiones*, VII.249, line 16.

[11] See §6 (ed. Migne, *Patrologia Latina*, L.1236). There is a modern text in Cavallin, *Vitae*. On this *Vita* see Kolon, *Die Vita*, especially p. 59f. Like Migne, *Patrologia Latina*, L.1237, n. *d*, and Kolon *Die Vita*, p. 64, I cannot explain the startling phrases *in discrimine uitae positus* and *custodibus appositis* in *Vita S. Hilarii*, §17 (ed. Migne, *Patrologia Latina*, L.1238).

[12] See especially §§16–17.

[13] Here is the Latin text: 'simul ingerentes [the informers] saeculi administratione perfunctum capitali aliquos condemnasse sententia. Tantae rei nouitate permoti [the two bishops], testes imperant praepari.' Notice the plural in *permoti* and *imperant*: the writer is speaking of Germanus as well as of Hilary. But the narrative then reverts to the singular: the rest of the story is about Hilary alone with no further reference to Germanus at any part of *Vita S. Hilarii* or of the other documents bearing on the episode.

The inference seems to me to be unwarranted. We know from Constantius[14] that when Germanus went to Arles to visit the Praetorian Prefect of Gaul, Auxiliaris, in the mid-thirties of the century,[15] he was warmly welcomed by Hilary. But Constantius says nothing about prolonged collaboration between the two clerics. He does not say that many years later they were still working together. Indeed, as Borius points out,[16] Constantius refers to Hilary in three very conventional lines,[17] with a distinct lack of warmth and fervour. But all that, to be sure, is a mere *argumentum ex silentio* upon which we must not lay much weight. Yet what we must particularly notice is that, although the *Vita* of Hilary of Arles tells how Germanus and Hilary began to obtain evidence against Celidonius, it gives no hint as to *when* they did so or how long it took them to obtain it. There is no date in the whole of this part of the *Vita S. Hilarii*. We do not know how long a time separated the beginning of the Celidonius affair from its culmination in the seventeenth *Novel*. The *Vita S. Hilarii* suppresses the fact that Pope Leo denounced Hilary in his *Epistle 10* and also that when he did so he had not one but three accusations to bring forward against the bishop of Arles. In fact, the Pope had delayed his denunciation against Hilary until he had much more than the affair of Celidonius to charge him with. Not only was his action against Celidonius unjustified, but he was equally wrong in his treatment of Proiectus (whose see, like his case, is unknown) and in his use of armed soldiers to impose priests on vacant churches. (We need not linger over these two latter charges; and indeed we have no chronological or other information about them.) In other words, the account of the incident given by the *Vita S. Hilarii* is a selective one: it tells of one only of the pope's complaints against Hilary and that, of course, is the one in which Hilary's position was strongest. It suppresses all mention of the pope's other two accusations and also of the fact that the pope championed Celidonius. Unhappily, the date of the pope's *Epistle 10* is unknown and it is mere guesswork to say that it can hardly be much earlier than Valentinian's *Novel 17*. The date when the entire affair began is therefore altogether unknown.

Indeed, the *Vita S. Hilarii* itself gives us a clear indication that the story was more complex than historians usually allow. After Hilary returned to Arles from his ill fated visit to Leo in Rome, negotiations between him and the pope had by no means come to an end. They continued through intermediaries. Hilary kept on trying to placate Leo, and he had first sent to Rome Ravennius, at that time a priest but afterwards his own successor in the see of Arles, and later on Nectarius of Avignon, and Constantius of Uzès, to negotiate on his behalf. These negotiations were not carried on in a hurry, and there may well have been other goings to and fro of which we hear nothing. Indeed, another of Hilary's intermediaries was that same Auxiliaris

[14] *Vita*, §23 (268,11).
[15] See p. 2 above.
[16] Borius, *Constance*, p. 96.
[17] *Vita*, §23 (268,10).

who had been Praetorian Prefect of Gaul in the mid-thirties. He was now City Prefect at Rome.[18] The author of the *Vita S. Hilarii*[19] quotes a tactful and delicately worded letter from Auxiliaris to Hilary, pointing out that 'men do not put up with it if we speak to them quite as we feel. The ears of the Romans are more attracted by a sensitiveness of language. If Your Sanctity were willing to accommodate yourself henceforth, you would lose nothing and would gain a great deal', and so on in a charming and most friendly style. I conclude that it is hazardous to use the *Vita S. Hilarii*[20] as proof that the whole story – from the decision to set in motion the machinery for collecting evidence against Celidonius to the publication of the *Novel* on 8 July 445 – took place within one year and that therefore Germanus was still alive in 444. His collaboration with Hilary, if it took place at all, may have ended years earlier. It might well be the case, for example, that Germanus and Hilary had discussed the position of Celidonius when Germanus visited Arles during the Prefecture of Auxiliaris in the mid-thirties. That is when the *Vita S. Germani* suggests that their collaboration was closest. But Germanus is not associated in any of our sources with the subsequent enquiry into Celidonius's past or with Hilary's denunciation of him or with his fight back against Hilary or with his appeal and journey to Rome and Hilary's subsequent negotiations with Leo, still less with Leo's deliberations on the case and his consultation with the Emperor. Leo makes no reference to Germanus in his *Epistle 10*. The Celidonius affair certainly came to a climax in 444/5, but no one knows when the first steps were taken; and it is only in connexion with the very earliest stage of the matter that Germanus's name is mentioned. It has also been pointed out that the florid, rhetorical *Vita S. Hilarii* is strongly biased in favour of Hilary; as Kolon remarks,[21] its author has a double aim – not to throw doubt on his praises of Hilary but at the same time to say nothing which might show Leo in a bad light. These two aims are hardly reconcilable. Such a document must be used with caution. It gives valuable information about the later stages of Hilary's negotiations with the pope through the intermediacy of Ravennius, Nectarius, Constantius, and the Prefect Auxiliaris. But the author is quite explicit about his desire to bring no discredit on two eminent men, Leo and Hilary, who are now dead.[22] In view of the scathing attack launched upon Hilary later on by Leo in connexion with the case of Celidonius – the Pope went as far as to call Hilary 'an habitual liar', *Hilarus pro more suo mentiri* – the author of the *Vita S. Hilarii* may have found it advisable to associate another eminent and highly revered bishop with Hilary, not because he was associated with him in fact, but so as

---

[18] See Jones *et al.*, *The Prosopography*, II.206, where Auxiliaris 1 and Auxiliaris 2 are almost certainly the same person. It is pointed out there that Auxiliaris can hardly have been Praetorian Prefect of Italy at the relevant time as that office was held by a certain Albinus from 443 to 449.
[19] §17 (ed. Migne, *Patrologia Latina*, L.1238f.).
[20] *Ibid.*, §16.
[21] Kolon, *Die Vita*, p. 64f.
[22] *Vita S. Hilarii*, §17 (ed. Migne, *Patrologia Latina*, L.1238).

to lend weight and respectability to Hilary's actions. Germanus may not have been seriously involved in the matter, and indeed some scholars go so far as to doubt whether he was concerned at all in the deposition of Celidonius.[23]

But to all this a critic might reply that it is not legitimate to deny the truth of a statement made by an ancient author merely because what he says does not square with some newfangled theory of our own. On the other hand, we should not be dismayed by the long delay – in clearing up the position of Celidonius – which is implied if we put the date of Germanus's death back to the 430s. It would be a mistake to forget that the speed of action of a bureaucracy, even of an ecclesiastical bureaucracy, is not always impressive. Admittedly, if we suppose that Hilary consulted with Germanus when Germanus was on his way to Ravenna in 437 (which is the year in which, as I shall suggest, Germanus died), then eight years is the minimum length of time over which the matter extended. No doubt other cases of delay by an ecclesiastical bureaucracy were even worse: for example, the bishop of Astigi (modern Ecija) in Spain was wrongly removed from his see in 625 and was unable to recover it for fifteen years!

The second matter which has led scholars to date the death of Germanus to the 440s arises from a passage of the *Vita* of Constantius[24] where we are told how the bishop of Auxerre restored life to the son of Volusianus, *cancellarius* of the patrician Sigisvult. (The *cancellarius* of an official was a sort of personal assistant who controlled access to him.) Now, it is certain that Sigisvult was not a patrician in the 430s. Valentinian III mentions him in two laws published in 440. In one of these he calls him *comes et magister utriusque militiae*, and in the other *uir illustrissimus magister militum*.[25] In neither law does he call him a patrician; and the reason can only be that at that date Sigisvult was not a patrician. Surely the inference must be that he became a patrician after 440, and, if so, that Germanus must have been alive after that year.

But in fact students of the period have raised serious objections to the patriciate of Sigisvult on grounds which have nothing to do with the career of Germanus. Apart from Constantius's *Life* of Germanus no authentic document makes him a patrician at any date.[26] It was the rule in Valentinian's reign that the patriciate was not bestowed on generals (as distinct from civilian officials) other than the supreme commander, who throughout this

[23] See Langgärtner, *Die Gallienpolitik*, p. 67 and n. 13, following Franses, *Paus Leo*, p. 36f. Dr Mathisen kindly gave me access to Franses's book. Unhappily, Kolon (*Die Vita*) expressed no opinion on the matter one way or the other.

[24] *Vita*, § 38 (278,1).

[25] *Nouella Valentiniani*, VI.1 (20 March 440); IX (24 June 440).

[26] Barnes, 'Patricii', pp. 163–5, has shown that the *Gesta de purgatione Xysti* should be disregarded as evidence for the reign of Valentinian III; cf. Levison, 'Bischof Germanus', p. 132, n. 6. Incidentally, it is hardly necessary to add that Sigisvult had a *cancellarius* attached to him by virtue of his being *magister militum* or consul, not because of his alleged patriciate.

period was Aetius. It has been shown, for example, that the poet and *magister utriusque militiae* Merobaudes was not a patrician.[27] No one must be on a par with Aetius, and to this rule the only exception that we hear of is Sigisvult, and, as I have said, for his patriciate there is no other evidence than this one passage of the *Vita S. Germani*. It is not impossible, therefore, that Constantius is in error here. It may be that he wrote *patricii* by a slip when he ought to have written *consulis*, for Sigisvult was one of the consuls of the year 437. But another explanation is also possible. It may be that he called Sigisvult 'patrician' as a sort of courtesy-title, for it was common practice among historians in the fifth and sixth centuries to give this title to one of the most prominent generals of the day irrespective of whether he held the title officially or not; and Demandt is able to cite several passages of ancient writers who confer the title on Stilicho, Marcellinus, Arinthaeus, and Syagrius, men who in fact were never patricians.[28] Whatever may have been the reason which led Constantius to write *patricii* here, I incline to the view that he did so by mistake.

But the question may well be asked: what is the point of raising all these somewhat farfetched objections to what our sources plainly tell us? Why suppose that the Celidonius affair lasted for seven or eight years instead of the one or two years which the evidence might be taken to suggest? Why ascribe a mistake to Constantius in the matter of Sigisvult's patriciate? Why not suppose that Germanus did indeed live on into the 440s, as scholars universally suppose? In a word, why go out of our way to look for difficulties?

The fact is that, if we allow Germanus to live on into the 440s, we shall have to accuse either Constantius or the author of the Gallic 'Chronicle of A.D. 452' of a monstrous piece of confusion, of a mistake so vast that in comparison with it the tiny slip of writing *patricii* for *consulis* would seem a very small one indeed. This hideous mistake, if we allowed it, would concern the revolt of the Armoricans in which Germanus became involved as soon as he returned home from his second visit to Britain. A delegation from the Armorican rebels called upon him, and he agreed to act as middleman between them and the Emperor. Presumably the Armoricans appealed to Germanus rather than to any of the numerous other bishops of Gaul because

[27] Sigisvult is held to have been a patrician by Stein, *Histoire*, I.599, n. 82 (cf. II.117, n. 2), by Levison, 'Bischof Germanus', p. 132, and by others; but see Ensslin, 'Zum Heermeisteramt', pp. 483–6, and the authoritative article of Barnes, '*Patricii*'. That Sigisvult was a patrician is held cautiously by Jones, *The Later Roman Empire*, I.176, 'This rank was rarely, if ever, granted to other generals'; Jones *et al.*, *The Prosopography*, II.757f.; Clover, *Flavius Merobaudes*, p. 36, 'likely, but not certainly'. Seeck in *Pauly's Realencyclopädie*, II A, 2279, *s.v.* 'Sigisvultus', says nothing of the patriciate and does not cite this passage of the *Vita S. Germani*. It was exceedingly rare for Seeck to overlook any of the ancient authors thus in his *Realencyclopädie* articles. Did he nod here, or did he omit the *Vita* deliberately? He does not seem to discuss the matter of Sigisvult's alleged patriciate in his *Geschichte des Untergangs*.

[28] A. Demandt, *Pauly's Realencyclopädie*, Supplementband, XII.661f., who also doubts the patriciate of Sigisvult.

they knew from his period of office among them[29] that he had some sympathy for, or at the least some understanding of, the cause for which they were fighting. And they were right. He did indeed take great pains to win them a pardon. But, as we have seen,[30] his sympathy in this connexion was not shared by his biographer, Constantius, whose language when he speaks of the Armoricans suggests unmitigated hostility on the writer's part.[31] The Armorican revolt in question was led by a man called Tibatto, and Aetius had ordered the barbarous Alans under their pagan King Goar to crush it. That is what Constantius tells us, but he is not our only source of information about the rebellion.

The revolt led by Tibatto is also mentioned in the 'Chronicle of A.D. 452'.[32] In 435, the chronicle tells us, a rebellion broke out under Tibatto's leadership. Under the year 436 the chronicle is silent about the affairs of Armorica; and in that year Aetius was hotly engaged against the Burgundians of the kingdom of Worms.[33] Under 437, however, the chronicle returns to the Armoricans. It tells us that in this year Tibatto was taken prisoner, the other leaders of the revolt were imprisoned or put to death, and the rebellion came to an end, *Bacaudarum commotio conquiescit.* Whatever conclusion we may finally come to about the chronology of the Gallic Chronicle, this date of 437 seems assured. The Armoricans were suppressed by Litorius, who then galloped at the head of his men through Auvergne and reached Narbonne in time to raise the Gothic siege of that city. This siege had begun in 436, and its raising is clearly dated by Hydatius to 437.[34] The suppression of Armorica, then, is securely dated to 437.

The words of the Gallic Chronicle suggest that the revolt of Tibatto passed through two stages in 435. (i) The revolt began, and the rebels declared their secession from the Roman Empire, as their predecessors had done in 409. (It is noteworthy that, although they seceded from the Empire in 435, they were not above using as an intermediary a bishop who had by no means seceded from the Empire and indeed was an ex-official of that Empire!) And then (ii) practically all the slaves in Gaul conspired together in a Bacaudic movement. But this later development was beside the point, as far as

[29] I am assuming the correctness of the opinion expressed by Jones *et al.*, *The Prosopography*, II.504, that Germanus had been *dux tractus Armoricani et Neruicani* in his earlier days. This is not wholly certain, but on any other view we must assume that Constantius has made a mistake in his wording at §1 (251,11). Also, if Germanus had no earlier connexion with Armorica why did the rebels appeal to him rather than to any other Gallic bishop? To that question, of course, it might be answered that Germanus was selected simply because he was the most respected bishop in the Gaul of his day (Sidonius, *Epistulae*, VIII.15) and even has an entry devoted to his *floruit* in the Gallic 'Chronicle of A.D. 452', §114 (ed. Mommsen, *Chronica Minora*, I. 660), to say nothing of his mention in the *Vita S. Hilarii*.

[30] See p. 51 above.

[31] *Vita*, §28 (271,6), §40 (280,3).

[32] §§117, 119 (ed. Mommsen, *Chronica Minora*, I.660).

[33] Jones *et al.*, *The Prosopography*, II.24f.; cf. Bury, *A History*, I.249.

[34] See Hydatius, *Chronicle*, §§107, 110 (ed. Mommsen, *Chronica Minora*, II.22f.); cf. Sidonius, *Carmina*, VII.246f. Hydatius would seem to be in error in saying that it was Aetius who raised the siege, unless he means simply that the work was done under his auspices.

Constantius was concerned, and he says nothing of any such extension of the movement. Be that as it may, if we suppose that Germanus died in the 440s we shall have to conclude that the author of the Gallic Chronicle completely misunderstood what happened in Armorica. We should have to suppose (as I did myself in earlier days)[35] that Tibatto managed to escape after his capture in 437 and was able to put himself once again at the head of the Armoricans and to lead them in yet another revolt. This is an assumption which a French scholar has rightly described as a 'solution désespérée'.[36] It is an assumption which entails convicting the author of the 'Chronicle of A.D. 452' of omitting to mention the renewed outbreak and the escape of Tibatto from imprisonment and of an outright mistake when he wrote those words *commotio conquiescit*. Otherwise, if Tibatto did not escape, it involves accusing the chronicler of an inexcusable chronological error, for he places the suppression of the revolt in the year preceding that of the publication of the Theodosian Code (438), whereas on this theory he ought to have placed it many years after that event. But this cannot be done, for his words are, as we have seen, supported by Hydatius and Sidonius. Alternatively, of course, we could assume that it was Constantius who made the mistake.[37] If Germanus died in the 440s his biographer has advanced the date of Tibatto's defeat by many years. Indeed, on this supposition one or other of the two authors who mention Tibatto by name has been guilty of an atrocious mistake in chronology.

Some scholars date the death of Germanus to 448: so, for example, Borius, the latest editor of Constantius, and also Loyen, who frankly calls Constantius's account 'un lapsus regrettable'.[38] Now, that same Gallic Chronicle does indeed report a Bacaudic movement in 448, but it gives no hint that that movement was led by Tibatto. As we have seen, that would be to misdate Tibatto's activities by no less than eleven years. And we do not know that the movement of 448 affected Armorica at all or whether it was confined to some other part of Gaul. Nor do we know that it resulted in a face-to-face confrontation, or any other kind of confrontation, with the Alans such as Constantius reports or that the Alans were in any way involved in it. Again, we know that in the months before Salvian wrote his *De Gubernatione Dei* in 440/1 the Bacaudae were attracting new recruits on an extensive scale: people were flying to them from every direction.[39] But Salvian does not suggest that the unrest of which he speaks culminated in fighting at that time

[35] Thompson, 'Britain', p. 311. For a new and fascinating theory about the end of Tibatto see Barnes, 'Merobaudes', p. 319, but even its author expresses some doubt about its validity.

[36] Loyen, 'L'oeuvre', p. 165, n. 3. Levison, 'Bischof Germanus', p. 139, calls this solution 'höchst bedenklich'.

[37] Levison, 'Bischof Germanus', p. 139, wonders whether Constantius has not converted Tibatto, who was the rebel leader in 435–7, into the leader of a later revolt. Which later revolt? Levison, *apud* Krusch & Levison, *Passiones*, VII.232, and in 'Bischof Germanus', p. 141, decided in the end that it was 'perhaps' that of 448. On this theory we have first to invent a later Armorican revolt and then to suppose that Tibatto was mistakenly regarded as the leader of it.

[38] Borius, *Constance*, p. 101; Loyen, 'L'oeuvre', p. 165.

[39] Salvian, *De Gubernatione Dei*, V.21f.

between the Bacaudae and the forces of the government. The situation was boiling up, but there had been no outbreak of actual warfare at the time of which he is speaking. And, once more, we do not know that this movement affected Armorica, a part of Gaul which Salvian never mentions by name.

Another fact to be taken into account is that at some date in these years Aetius settled a band of Alans – the Alans of Goar – in northern Gaul, apparently near Orléans.[40] It is usually assumed that this settlement dates from 442, the first time when we hear of these Alans. The inference has been drawn that Armorica was in revolt in 442. But, as a matter of fact, we do not know when these barbarians were planted in Gallia Ulterior. What the 'Chronicle of A.D. 452'[41] reports is a revolt of the Roman landowners of the locality against these Alan settlers in 442. The settlement itself may, for all we know, have been carried through directly after the suppression of the Armoricans in 437. That is only a guess: the date of the settlement is not known exactly, although it is unlikely to have been carried out very long before the revolt of the landowners of the area. The arrival of the ferocious Alan nomads[42] will not have been slow to cause trouble. The settlement was in all probability arranged when Aetius was still present in Gaul: so striking a move as the planting of a group of savage barbarians in Gallia Ulterior in virtual autonomy could hardly have been planned and executed in the great man's absence. And this is particularly true in view of the nomadic character of Alan society. It was wholly contrary to Imperial practice in the West to settle nomads inside the frontier for the obvious reason that their way of life would be entirely alien to that of the provincials around them. These Alans are one of the exceptional cases. They had crossed the Rhine into Gaul in 406 in company with the Vandals and Sueves, and there was no means of forcing them to leave the Empire again. (Later on, the government discovered a method: it set the Visigoths on to the majority of them in Spain and so caused them to be all but annihilated.[43]) I should suggest that Aetius, before leaving Gaul and returning to Italy in 439,[44] had planted the Alans in the neighbourhood of Orléans, perhaps directly after the war of 437. (If that is true, we must not say that Goar and his men were marching from Orléans on their way to crush the Armoricans when Germanus encountered them:[45] we do not know where they were coming from.) At all events, the action of the Alans and the landowners in 442 provides no evidence whatever for a rebellion of

[40] Jordanes, *Getica*, § 194.

[41] § 127 (ed. Mommsen, *Chronica Minora*, I.660).

[42] For the nomadic society of the Alans see especially Ammianus Marcellinus, *History*, XXXI.2. They were on a much lower level of material development than the major Germanic peoples. Note *Vita*, § 28 (271,7), *Gochari ferocissimo Alanorum regi*; Salvian, *De Gubernatione Dei*, IV.68, *rapacitas Alani*. Such a people would show little regard for the niceties of *hospitalitas*. For a general study of them see Bachrach, *A History*.

[43] Note how few nomadic peoples are to be found in the magnificent list, of barbarian peoples settled inside the Roman empire, drawn up by de Ste. Croix, *The Class Struggle*, pp. 508–19.

[44] 'Chronicle of A.D. 452', § 123 (ed. Mommsen, *Chronica Minora*, I.660).

[45] Borius, *Constance*, p. 102.

the Armoricans in or after 442 with which we could associate Tibatto and Germanus. After 437 peace descended on Armorica: that part of Gaul is, as I said, not mentioned by Salvian. When the poet Merobaudes celebrated Aetius's third consulate on 1 January 446 he says explicitly that the Armorican region is 'now' quiet, the implication being that at a former date (perhaps 435–7) it had been far from quiet.[46] To what extent, if any, this peace was due to the presence of the Alans near Orléans is unknown and is beside the point for our purpose. In 451 Armorica was independent of the Roman government altogether, and so it remained for the rest of West Roman history.[47]

Thus, although we are by no means ill informed about Armorica in the period 435–51, we know of no sequence of events with which the circumstances described by Constantius could be identified except those of 435–7. Any other hypothesis must necessarily entail ascribing a chronological howler to Constantius or to the Chronicler of A.D. 452.

I suggest that Tibatto rebelled in 435, as the Chronicler tells us that he did, and that no action was taken against him in 436 because Aetius was deeply engaged with the Burgundians of the kingdom of Worms in that year: hence the silence of the Chronicle concerning Armorica in 436. Germanus visited Britain for the second time in the spring of 437 and spent only a short time there. He had scarcely reached Auxerre on his return[48] when a deputation from Armorica persuaded him to intervene to stop the war which was now on the point of breaking out afresh, for in this year Aetius was able to spare the cavalry of King Goar for action in the far West. According to Constantius, Germanus then went on a leisurely journey[49] to Italy, reached Milan by 19 June,[50] fell sick on 25 July,[51] and died on the last day of the month (although Constantius does not give us that date). The *Vita* informs us that the saint would have won a permanent peace for Armorica had not Tibatto renewed the revolt, nullified the bishop's efforts, and quickly (*breui*) paid the penalty:[52] that is to say, Tibatto was defeated in the summer – say, August or September – of 437. In this way the evidence of the 'Chronicle of

---

[46] Merobaudes, *Panegyric*, II.8.

[47] There are a few remarks on this subject in Thompson, 'Procopius', p. 502f.

[48] *Vita*, § 28 (271,4), *uixdum domum*.

[49] *Ibid.*, § 33 (275,6), 'dum iter sensim moris felicibus carpit', and it was only after leaving Milan that he put on speed, 'interea gradum accelerant', *ibid.*, § 34 (275,27).

[50] On this date see Grosjean, 'Notes', p. 181f., followed by Borius, *Constance*, p. 104. I have not followed Meslin, in his review of Borius, who suggests that the date here is the *natalis omnium martyrum*, the first Friday after Easter, although this is accepted by Mathisen, 'The last year', p. 156, n. 22. This would bring Germanus to Milan by the end of April at latest; and that would imply that he had left Auxerre by the end of February at latest, for we shall see (p. 66 below) that the journey from Auxerre to Ravenna probably took sixty days or thereabouts. On this hypothesis, then, the journey to Britain would have taken place in the autumn of the year preceding that of the visit to Ravenna. I have said (p. 56 above) that such a theory would not be easy to refute. But can we allow that the saint spent some twelve weeks or more in the capital?

[51] *Vita*, § 42 (281,10).

[52] *Ibid.*, § 40 (280,5).

A.D. 452' can be easily and completely reconciled with that which Constantius gives us in the *Vita*, and both Constantius and the Chronicler are saved from the outrageous mistake with which we must otherwise charge them.

We can make these dates somewhat more precise. It seems to have taken Germanus's body fifty-two days to reach Auxerre from Ravenna.[53] Since his journey from Auxerre to Milan was a leisurely one, let us suppose that he spent sixty days on the road to Ravenna, that is, that he left Auxerre about 20 April. He had just returned from Britain when the Armorican delegation called upon him. Say that he had been at home for a fortnight before he set out for Italy. In that case he would have left Britain about the first week in April, a week or two earlier than in 429. In this way we have a crowded programme for the saint in the spring and early summer of 437. If it should be thought to be too crowded, it might be possible to place the journey to Britain and the meeting with Goar in 436 and the journey to Ravenna to 437, although some may think that this distribution of the burden is too lenient to the saint. Scholars who spread the load over two years (de Plinval, Meslin) have been mentioned above.[54] They may well be right.

If we suppose that Germanus died at Ravenna in 437, a number of other matters, too, falls into place, although none of them is of decisive importance.

The last event which Constantius mentions before describing Germanus's second visit to Britain is the saint's encounter with Auxiliaris, Praetorian Prefect of Gaul.[55] He wished the Prefect to reduce the taxes of Auxerre, and I previously accepted the view of Levison that Auxiliaris's reduction of these taxes, reported in the *Vita*, could be identified with a more general reduction of the Gallic taxes which is recorded by Salvian as having been granted 'recently'.[56] Even though Salvian seems to have been writing *ca* 440/1 so that his 'recently', *nuper*, might well refer to the period 435–9, yet the language which the two authors use does not suggest that they have in mind one and the same event.[57] The affair of the taxes is the only matter which Constantius records from the period between the two British visits. He writes as though this matter arose immediately on the return of Germanus from his first visit to Britain – indeed, that it had already arisen in his absence on that journey and was awaiting his attention as soon as he reached home. This may be an overstatement on Constantius's part, implying that the bishop could not leave his diocese even for a short time without difficulties arising with which no one else was capable of dealing. In this case the difficulty confronting the

---

[53] Levison, 'Bischof Germanus', p. 100; or sixty days, according to Gregory of Tours, *Gloria Confessorum*, §40.
[54] See p. 56 above.
[55] *Vita*, §24 (268,13).
[56] Salvian, *De Gubernatione Dei*, V.35. See Grosjean, 'Notes', p. 135; [Krusch &] Levison, *Passiones*, VII.269, n. 2; Levison, 'Bischof Germanus', p. 125.
[57] The two remissions of taxes are distinguished by Jones *et al.*, *The Prosopography*, II.206, *s.n.* 'Auxiliaris 1', and with that opinion I should now agree.

citizens was a *tributaria functio praeter solitum*.[58] The rate of tax was announced each year by the Praetorian Prefect and became known to the provinces perhaps by 1 July (although the date specifically for Gaul is unknown). The complaint in the present passage may be that the rate of levy was felt to be oppressively high in this year (for the rate varied from year to year). It might be thought that what the citizens were complaining of was a superindiction. But the prefect normally had to obtain the Emperor's permission to impose a superindiction and only an emergency could justify one. But if that had been the case in this instance it is unlikely that Auxiliaris would have been prepared to remit the additional demand so light-heartedly when Germanus asked him to do so. It is improbable that, if he had obtained the Emperor's permission to impose a superindiction, he would now write lamely and tell the Emperor that after all a superindiction was unnecessary. (Observe that the tax-relief secured by Germanus from the prefect was relief for his own *ciuitas* only, not for his province,[59] although that hardly proves that the impost was limited to Auxerre alone.) But in addition to the regular tax the citizens had apparently also been called upon for supplementary levies: that seems to be implied by the words *et necessitates innumerae*.[60]

But what concerns us in particular is the chronology of the affair. An inscription on a milestone erected on the road from Arles to Marseilles informs us that Auxiliaris was holding his office at some date when Theodosius II was consul for the fifteenth time, that is, after 1 January 435, and before the emperor held the consulate for the sixteenth time, which he began to do on 1 January 438.[61] We know also that Auxiliaris was no longer in this office in 439, for in that year Eparchius Avitus, the future Emperor, held it.[62] That is to say, the meeting of Auxiliaris and Germanus took place in or perhaps before 435 but certainly not later than 438.[63] These are the last recorded events in the saint's career before his departure for his second visit to Britain. If we date that visit to 437, then the journey to Auxiliaris will fall in 436 or a year or two earlier; but if we date it to 448, then there is a gap of a decade or so in our knowledge of Germanus's life. That, of course, is not a valid reason in itself for accepting 437 rather than 448 as the date of the visit to Britain.

But let us look a little more closely at the language which Constantius uses here. He is notoriously vague in chronology, as we have all too good reason to know. He says that Germanus set out to meet Auxiliaris *ca* 435, as we have

[58] *Vita*, §19 (265,16).

[59] *Ibid.*, §24 (269,12).

[60] On the whole subject see Jones, *The Later Roman Empire*, I.451f.

[61] Dessau, *Inscriptiones*, no. 806.

[62] Jones *et al.*, *The Prosopography*, II.197f., citing Sidonius, *Carmina*, VII.295–8, with Hydatius, *Chronicle*, §117 (ed. Mommsen, *Chronica Minora*, II.23).

[63] Borius, *Constance*, p. 94 (cf. p. 96 *ad fin.*), dates the journey to Auxiliaris to 430/1 or 'towards 430', which seems too early since it implies an abnormally long tenure of the office by Auxiliaris: see Jones, *The Later Roman Empire*, I.380. Exceptionally long tenures of this office are not wholly unknown, but there is no obvious reason why the Emperor should have made an exception of Auxiliaris.

just seen. When he returned, *interea*[64] news came from Britain that Pelagianism had revived there, so that he set out for that island *festinus*, 'in a hurry'.[65] Scarcely had he returned home from Britain (*uixdum domum*)[66] when the Armorican legation met him. Is it not difficult to allow that any writer, however cloudy his notions of time, would have used such language (*interea, festinus, uixdum*) if ten or even thirteen years had elapsed between the return from Auxiliaris and the arrival of the Armorican legation (*ca* 435–48 on this theory)? To suppose that this is the case is to think, not that Constantius's chronological terms are vague, but that his language is altogether meaningless. On the other hand, if the events mentioned here covered no more than two or three years (435–7), then Constantius's expressions are very reasonable and apt.

Let us look now at Germanus after he had arrived in Ravenna. If we linger over Constantius's account of the interest taken by the Imperial family in the saint when he had arrived in the capital we shall notice a fact of no small importance. When Germanus first reached Ravenna he was welcomed by Placidia (the Emperor's mother) and Valentinian III as well as by Peter Chrysologus,[67] the bishop of Ravenna. The Empress sent a huge silver dish to Germanus at his inn.[68] He in turn sent her a little wooden plate for which she was grateful.[69] Somewhat later a protégé of Acolius, *praepositus sacri cubiculi*, a young man who was subject to fits, was handed over to Germanus by 'the Empress and the leading men'.[70] When Germanus fell sick, the Empress enquired after the invalid and gave him whatever he wanted.[71] When he died, the Empress took his reliquary[72] and also provided a shroud for his corpse.[73] After the initial welcome by the Emperor and his mother, the Emperor drops completely out of the story, and Placidia alone takes part in the subsequent events. Now, if we take 437 to be the year in which all this happened, there was a very good reason why Valentinian should disappear from the picture: on 15 July, according to the *Annals of Ravenna*, he set sail (from Rome, as we hear elsewhere) for Constantinople to marry Eudoxia.[74]

---

[64] Observe the remark of Anderson on Sidonius, *Carmina*, VII.230: 'It is important to note that *interea* is often used in poetry to introduce a new action subsequent to, not contemporaneous with, the events just described. . . . "meanwhile" is often a misleading translation'. In the passage on which he is commenting Anderson renders the word by 'anon'. These facts refute important arguments of Miller, 'Bede's use'.

[65] *Vita*, §25 (269,17).

[66] *Ibid.*, §28 (271,4).

[67] *Ibid.*, §35 (276,11–15).

[68] *Ibid.* (276,17).

[69] *Ibid.* (277,2f.).

[70] *Ibid.*, §39 (279,13).

[71] *Ibid.*, §42 (281,5).

[72] *Ibid.*, §43 (281,15).

[73] *Ibid.*, §44 (282,2).

[74] The *Annals of Ravenna* were first published by Bischoff & Koehler, 'Eine illustrierte Ausgabe', from which I quote. On p. 128 we read: 'Aetio II et Segiuul. his consulibus Valentinianus nauigauit ad orientem id. Iul. die Iouis hora iii et accepit uxorem u kal. Nouemb.'. That he sailed from Rome is mentioned by Marcellinus Comes, *Chronicle, s.a.* 437 (ed. Mommsen, *Chronica Minora*, II.79).

That accounts for the fact that he was present to welcome Germanus on his arrival, but took no part in later contacts with him. The breakdown of the saint's negotiations with the government on behalf of the Armoricans does not entail the presence of Valentinian in person in Ravenna, and indeed the negotiations may have broken down before 15 July.[75] And when we are told that after the saint's death 'the Emperor' paid for the homeward journey of the corpse and provided the *euectiones* (the warrants which would allow it and its attendants to travel by the public post), we must bear in mind that it did not take the Emperor in person to put up the relatively tiny sum of money involved – and indeed the *euectiones* were supplied by an official of the Praetorian Prefecture: they were not signed by the Emperor's own hand.[76] Stewart Oost saw to the heart of this matter (although he went too far in thinking that the Emperor was in Rome throughout the whole time of Germanus's stay in Ravenna: he was undoubtedly present in Ravenna when the saint arrived there):[77] 'Since it is incredible that the emperor, Placidia's son, if present, would have paid no similar attention to the saint, we may conclude that he was not present, for no such attention is recorded'.[78] If we choose some year other than 437 as the date of Germanus's visit to Ravenna, we shall have to assume that the absence of Valentinian from the later part of the saint's stay is an unexplained coincidence. But that, of course, is not to say that it is an impossibility.

But there are one or two other points which seem clearly to support a date in the 430s rather than the 440s as the time of Germanus's death. None of them is conclusive, although none is negligible. When Germanus reached Ravenna, the Western Empire, according to Constantius, was ruled by *Placidia regina cum filio Valentiniano iam iuuene*.[79] What is the meaning of *iam iuuene*? The words are a satisfactory description of a young man of the Imperial family who had been born on 2 July 419 and was now (if the reference is to the summer of 437) exactly eighteen years of age. But if Constantius is speaking of the summer of 444 or of some other year down to 448, then Valentinian was 25 or even 29 years old; and in that case *iam iuuene* is decidedly less apposite. No young man of 25 (to say nothing of 29) would feel flattered at being called *iam iuuene* – and Constantius's attitude here, if not one of flattery, is certainly one of respect for the nominal Emperor. Secondly, in those same words Constantius mentions the Emperor's mother as well as the Emperor himself, but he says nothing of the Emperor's wife. Yet on 21 October 437 Valentinian entered Constantinople. On 28 October he

---

[75] Constantius tells us of the collapse of the negotiations in strangely abstract language: 'imperialis credulitas circumscriptione frustrata est'; *Vita* § 40 (280,4).

[76] Jones, *The Later Roman Empire*, II.587.

[77] *Vita*, § 35 (276,14).

[78] Oost, *Galla Placidia*, p. 255, who writes *ibid.*, p. 254, n. 13, about the payment for the return of the corpse and the issue of the *euectiones* that 'undoubtedly his mother felt free to use the facilities of the court or state with or without her son's specific permission'.

[79] *Vita*, § 35 (276,13). Constantius uses the phrase *iam iuuenis* again in *Vita*, § 39 (279,10).

married Licinia Eudoxia there,[80] and brought her back to Ravenna in the spring of 438. Constantius may have omitted mention of Eudoxia because she could not be said to be 'ruling' in the sense in which the forceful and formidable Placidia was ruling, but it would have been tactful to mention her and rather disrespectful to omit her altogether if she had been present. I should suggest that he omitted to mention her because at the time of which he is speaking Valentinian had not yet married her. Further, as we have seen, Constantius stresses the interest which the Imperial family showed in his hero, both alive and dead. Is it possible to believe that the biographer would have passed over Licinia Eudoxia in complete silence if she had already been married to Valentinian III and was displaying an interest in the holy man of Auxerre? I think that, if she had been present in Ravenna, Constantius would not have failed to speak of her. On the other hand, she may have been absent from the capital for some wholly irrelevant reason.

What are we to conclude then about the date of Germanus's death? Whether we date it to 437 or to the 440s we are obliged to ascribe a mistake to one or other of our authorities. But no explanation of any problem in ancient history can be wholly satisfactory if it entails supposing that one of our authorities is wrong – that since an ancient author does not tell us what we want him to tell us or what we think that he ought to have told us, *therefore* he must be wrong, he must have made a mistake. But in the present case there seems to be no way of avoiding such a supposition. Whichever date we choose, we encounter evidence which will not square with our theory. The evidence, in fact, is self-contradictory. *Either* Constantius has erred in calling Sigisvult a patrician *or else* he, or perhaps the Chronicler of 452, has made an atrocious muddle of the chronology of the Armorican revolt. I should choose the lesser mistake. To call Sigisvult a patrician instead of a consul (especially when other authors are so generous in bestowing patriciates on men who never were patricians) seems a more pardonable mistake, and easier to account for, than that one or other of our authorities was utterly mistaken about the time of the Armorican revolt, especially given the evidence of Sidonius.

If we accept the hypothesis that 437 is the year in question we shall be able to understand Constantius's indications of time – *interea, festinus, uixdum* – when otherwise we should have to convict him of a gross misuse of language. We can understand why Valentinian III was able to welcome Germanus to Ravenna but not to take any further part in his activities there. We can see why Constantius uses the phrase *iam iuuene* of the Emperor,[81] which on any other interpretation would be misleading or even insulting, and why he makes no reference to Licinia Eudoxia, which would be an offensive omission were he speaking of some year in the 440s. These points, taken collectively, carry some weight, although they do not amount to proof. We cannot account for them if the second visit to Britain is dated to the 440s.

[80] *Annals of Ravenna, s.a.* 437 (edd. Bischoff & Koehler, p. 128), although the date is October 29 in Marcellinus Comes, *Chronicle, s.a.* 437 (ed. Mommsen, *Chronica Minora*, II.79).
[81] See p. 68f. above.

VIII

ARMORICA

We must beware of equating the Latin term 'Armorica' with the modern Brittany. The *Tractus Armoricanus* included Brittany, to be sure, but it included a great deal more besides. Within its boundaries lay the whole of France between the Garonne and a line drawn somewhat east of the Seine. Its easternmost part was made up of the province of Lugdunensis Senonia, of which the capital was Sens and which included Paris, Chartres, Troyes, Orléans, and among other places Auxerre. Auxerre was part of Armorica, and it has often been held that Germanus of Auxerre had once held the office of *dux tractus Armoricani*.

In 435–7 the *Tractus Armoricanus* was in revolt,[1] but we cannot accept that all of it had risen. It is out of the question that the province of Aquitanica Secunda (between the Garonne and the lower reaches of the Loire) had rebelled, for the Visigoths had been planted there as Federates in 418 and would have opposed any such uprising. Again, there is no sign of revolt at Auxerre where an Armorican deputation called on Germanus. But the revolt was nonetheless an enormous one, and several contemporary writers refer to it.

Constantius gives us information of capital interest about it, but it is information about the impact which the revolt made on the outside world. He does not take us into the interior of Armorica and introduce us to the rebels and their cause. It is a pity that he does not tell us more, but we must examine what he does tell us and see what we can make of it.

He is not our only source of information about this rebellion. The Gallic 'Chronicle of A.D. 452' also speaks of it, and Sidonius Apollinaris[2] not only helps to confirm the date of its suppression[3] but also adds what Constantius omitted to say (because it was irrelevant to his theme as a hagiographer) – that in the end it was the Count Litorius, with a force of Hunnish cavalry, who crushed the rebellion. What had become of Goar and his Alans in this connexion, we do not know.

Germanus had scarcely returned home from the second visit to Britain,

---

[1] See pp. 61–6 above.
[2] Sidonius, *Carmina*, VII.247f.
[3] See p. 62 above.

uixdum domum . . . remeauerat,[4] when a 'delegation' – *legatio*, the same word which he had used of the British delegation in 429[5] – from the *Tractus Armoricanus* solicited his help. We are eager to learn at once why this deputation called upon him and what exactly they wanted the holy man to do; but this we are never told. We learn instead the motive of Aetius for acting as he had done: offended at the insolence of that haughty region he had given permission to the Alan nomad-horsemen under their pagan king, Goar, to suppress the rebels. In other words, Constantius is interested in telling us why Aetius acted as he did. He is not interested in telling us why the Armoricans acted as they did (a more interesting theme, some may think). In fairness to him we must bear in mind that it might not have been easy for one writing in 480–90 to find out the motives of the Celtic-speaking Armoricans for acting as they had half a century before. But it is more likely that he was not deterred by the difficulty of finding out their motives, but rather by his indifference to what their motives had been for seceding from the Empire. It is from the Gallic 'Chronicle of A.D. 452'[6] that we learn the aim of the rebels: they aimed at secession from the Roman empire. That is to say, this was a continuation of the Armorican independence-movement of 409, the year in which the Armoricans, imitating the Britons (as we have seen),[7] expelled the Roman officials and lived in independence until they were suppressed by Exuperantius in 417. What Exuperantius achieved in 417 was fourfold. (i) He taught Armorica to love the return of peace from her captivity among the enemy. (ii) He reimposed Roman law upon the Armoricans. (iii) He brought back freedom. (iv) 'He does not allow them to be the slaves of their own slaves', *et seruos famulis non sinit esse suis*.[8] Many scholars ignore this line: perhaps they believe that you cannot expect a poet to tell the truth, particularly when he is writing a pentameter. But, in fact, there is no reason to doubt that this pentameter means what it says, and that the Armoricans had carried out (in imitation of the Britons) an important social revolution of a kind unparalleled (as far as we know) in the Western Roman empire before 409. What Exuperantius did was to restore Imperial rule. The 'freedom' which he brought back from her captivity was the freedom of the landowners. There is no reason why the Armorican revolt of 435–7 should have had different aims from those of 409; indeed, in one respect, that of secession, we know that the aims of both movements were identical. But we have seen[9] that no one other than the rural poor would wish to secede, and it was they who carried out the programme which we can deduce from those

---

[4] *Vita*, § 28 (271,5).
[5] *Ibid.*, § 12 (259,5).
[6] § 117 (ed. Mommsen, *Chronica Minora*, I.660).
[7] See p. 35 above.
[8] Rutilius Namatianus, *De Reditu Suo*, I.216. The difficulties, such as they are, of this passage are exaggerated by Bartholomew, 'Fifth-century facts', pp. 266–8. See the commentary by Doblhofer, *Rutilius*, II.177.
[9] See p. 34 above.

lines of Rutilius Namatianus. If anyone would argue that, apart from the objective of secession, the revolt of 435–7 differed from that of 409, the burden of proof rests most decidedly upon him.

But, when Constantius speaks of what the Armoricans and their opponents did, he discusses none of these things. He speaks of the Armoricans' 'insolence'. He calls them 'haughty'. He mentions their 'presumption'[10] and Tibatto's and the people's 'perfidy'. He calls the people 'fickle and undisciplined'.[11] Where other writers give us facts, he gives us abuse. He sees the whole incident from the outside. He sees it from the point of view of Aetius and the Imperial government. He does not regard Tibatto as having a point of view or, at any rate, one which is worth mentioning. The audience for which he was writing would by no means have found inspiration or edification in the policies of Tibatto. A major problem is why Germanus felt differently about the Armorican revolt. We shall discuss the question later on.[12]

At the end of his book Constantius apologises for not telling all that he knew about the saint. It is a normal cliché of the hagiographers.[13] But he does give us clear evidence to show that in one matter of the first importance he has been guilty of an omission so monstrous that it is hard to forgive him for it. At the end of the famous scene in which Germanus caught hold of the savage Goar's bridle and refused to allow him to advance farther against the Armoricans, he tells us that Goar agreed to call off his campaign but that he would only do so on one condition: the bishop must obtain an amnesty for the rebels *ab imperatore uel ab Aetio*.[14] The rest of the book goes on to give a lively, vivid, credible, and invaluable account of the saint's journey across Gaul and the Alps to Ravenna. (He travels in a peace, by the way, which seems on the surface to be as orderly and as unbroken as if the Empire were still ruled by Augustus or Trajan.) He travels in order to obtain such an amnesty *ab imperatore*. But what about those words *uel ab Aetio*? A number of scholars, including the two translators, Borius[15] and Hoare,[16] have been misled by Classical Latin usage. In Classical Latin, of course, *uel* universally means 'or', and they have taken Goar to mean that either the Emperor or Aetius must amnesty the Armoricans. But in Late Latin (from the fourth century onwards) *uel* no longer universally means 'or'. It commonly, though not always, means 'and'.[17] Now, in Constantius's *Vita* the word occurs fifteen times (including the passage under discussion), and on every occasion without exception it means 'and'. There is no variation except –

---

[10] *Vita*, §28 (271,6f.).
[11] *Ibid.*, §40 (280.3 & 6).
[12] See p. 77 below.
[13] *Vita*, §46 (283,5). Similarly, Sulpicius Severus, *Vita S. Martini*, I.8, tells us that he has omitted *plura*, while Eugippius, *Vita S. Seuerini*, Preface, 2, claims to have recorded no more than *aliqua indicia*.
[14] *Vita*, §28 (272,16).
[15] Borius, *Constance*, p. 177 (cf. p. 102).
[16] *The Western Fathers*, p. 309.
[17] In fact, the word eventually disappeared from the Latin language, the modern French 'ou', Spanish and Italian 'o', being *aut*.

although in fact these are not exceptions – where it means 'even',[18] and where *uel . . . uel* means 'both . . . and'.[19] In Constantius's text *uel* never means 'or' or 'beziehungsweise' or anything of the sort. It means 'and' and nothing but 'and'. Try translating the following passages, rendering *uel* as 'or', and you will find yourself in many a muddle: 'clerici omnes cunctaque nobilitas, plebs urbana uel rustica in unum uenere sententiam';[20] 'cum tali pontifice uel magistro';[21] 'se uel conparem suum auctores criminum fuisse multorum';[22] 'et casu dux uel pontifex, fractus corpore, lassitudine et sopore resolutus est';[23] 'interea haec constitutio uel forma castrorum hostibus nuntiatur';[24] 'interuentu reginae uel procerum sancto uiro praesentatur'.[25] In each of these and other cases, to render *uel* as 'or' would be not merely wrong, but comically wrong. There can be no reasonable doubt that Constantius is telling us that Goar offered a firm peace to the Armoricans provided that Germanus obtained an amnesty *both* from the Emperor *and* from Aetius. Since we do not know for certain in which year these events took place, we cannot know where Aetius was at the time in question. We do know, however, that, when Germanus reached Ravenna, Aetius was not present in the capital. In many of the possible years he was in Gaul at the relevant season. I am inclined to think that Germanus died in 437;[26] and presumably the patrician was busy in June and July of that year in organising the ferocious attack of the Huns on the Burgundian kingdom of Worms which caused such fearful casualties to the Burgundians and which was never forgotten in mediaeval Germanic poetry.[27] But if he was in Gaul he was much more accessible than the Emperor in Ravenna. He was well known, and was clearly known to Constantius, to be the real ruler of the West at that date – *Aetius qui tum rem publicam gubernabat.*[28] We might have thought, therefore, that Germanus, acting on behalf of the Armoricans, would approach Aetius first and the Emperor second.

Nothing in the narrative so far prepares us for what follows: although Goar had said, and Constantius reports him as saying, that Germanus must obtain an amnesty from both Valentinian and Aetius, Constantius seems immediately to forget about Aetius. He goes on as if he had never mentioned him. He never speaks of him or refers to him again. According to his narrative,

[18] *Vita*, Preface (248,14; 249,15); § 18 (265,2); § 23 (268,3).
[19] *Ibid.*, § 14 (260,24); § 18 (265,8).
[20] *Ibid.* § 2 (252,2).
[21] *Ibid.* (254,6).
[22] *Ibid.*, § 10 (258,6).
[23] *Ibid.*, § 13 (260,8).
[24] *Ibid.*, § 17 (264,11).
[25] *Ibid.*, § 39 (279,13). The other references are Preface (250,7); § 3 (252,15); § 10 (258,6); § 19 (265,19); § 22 (267,10). On the usage see Svennung, *Untersuchungen*, p. 495f.; Hofmann & Szantyr, *Lateinische Syntax*, p. 502.
[26] See p. 65 above.
[27] Prosper, *Chronicon*, § 1322 (ed. Mommsen, *Chronica Minora*, I.475); Gallic 'Chronicle of A.D. 452', § 118 (*ibid.*, I.660); and for the date Hydatius, § 110 (*ibid.*, II.23). In general and for bibliography see Clover, *Flavius Merobaudes*, p. 45, n. 43.
[28] *Vita*, § 28 (271,6).

Germanus made no attempt whatever to approach the patrician. The saint acted, according to what Constantius tells us, as though Aetius was not concerned in the case of the Armoricans, a point of view which might have surprised Goar and would certainly have astonished Aetius himself. In fact, Germanus had good reason to avoid Aetius's company. Had he not persuaded Goar to disobey point-blank, in the crudest possible manner, the explicit orders of the patrician? Would it not be true to say that he had wrecked one of the commander-in-chief's major military plans for the campaigning season of 437 (or whatever the year may have been)? If Aetius could have laid hands on the bishop, he would have had good reason for placing him under arrest! Perhaps it was fortunate that he was not in Ravenna when Germanus arrived there!

But if Constantius did not intend to narrate the approach of Germanus to Aetius, or to explain the absence of such an approach, is it not odd that he did not delete those three little words from his narrative – *uel ab Aetio*? Then the narrative would have run very smoothly – at some cost in accuracy, to be sure. It might be objected that Germanus intended to go on to interview Aetius when once he had persuaded the authorities in Ravenna to amnesty the rebels; but such an objection is pure speculation and will hardly convince. Assuming that Aetius was in Gaul at the time, it would be natural to approach him first. After all, he was the real ruler of the West; and if the bishop was successful with him, he could hardly expect opposition in Ravenna. It was Aetius's voice which counted, not Placidia's.

My own view is that Constantius's omission to tell us why Germanus did not contact Aetius on the subject of the amnesty is a non-problem. If we blame Constantius for this omission we are judging him as though he were writing a biography rather than hagiography. His purpose is to glorify his hero and to edify his readers – the point cannot be repeated too often – and for this purpose it was enough that he should take the saint to the capital of the Western world and show how he mixed with the members of the Imperial family, even with the Emperor himself, and how he was treated with respect and reverence by them. This was of immeasurably greater consequence than a description of any difficulties that he may have had with Aetius. *We* should like to know Aetius's attitude towards the amnesty, but we do not know whether Constantius's readers had much interest in any such thing.

That is far from being the end of our problems concerning the Armorican revolt. There are other matters, too, which are very obscure, although for Constantius's purpose it was probably beside the point to go into them just as it was beside the point to discuss Aetius's attitude towards an amnesty of the rebels. It is not at all clear, for example, why the Armoricans should have renewed their revolt when Germanus was in the very act of negotiating an amnesty with the government at Ravenna. After all, it was the Armoricans who had invited him to intervene. Moreover, they had won a major victory against the government not only when Germanus stopped the advance of Goar and the Alans but even before that, when they had made Goar's invasion necessary: they had overpowered such military forces as were stationed in their country and had (presumably) put down the resistance of the landowners, who would not have had any taste for secession. And when Goar withdrew as a result of his interview with Germanus, the Armoricans were left in complete, unchallenged control of their country with a guaranteed freedom from attack for as many weeks or months as it would take Germanus to complete his negotiations in Ravenna. In these months they could have consolidated their position, increased their stock of arms, stirred up revolt in other parts of Gaul, and so on. Why did they throw their opportunity away? Why did they compel the government to renew its attack on them? For Constantius, of course, it was beside the point to explain their motives. He merely says that they were 'fickle and undisciplined', *mobilem et indisciplinatum populum*:[29] that is merely telling us in different words that they had no consistent policy.

Again, Goar called off his attack on condition that Germanus should obtain from Valentinian III and Aetius that same *uenia*,[30] that same 'pardon', which Germanus had himself granted to them. But what could such 'pardon' amount to? Armorica had seceded from the Roman Empire, *a romana societate discessit*.[31] Did Germanus and Goar and the Armoricans expect to persuade Valentinian to acknowledge the secession and to recognise the freedom of Gallia Ulterior? No Roman emperor could do such a thing. When Britain seceded in 409, Honorius is certainly not recorded to have recognised the freedom of the Britons. Indeed, by writing to the British *ciuitates* in 410, bidding them defend themselves,[32] he implied that he still had the right to tell the Britons what they ought and ought not to do. Did Germanus, then, expect the Gallic slaves to go back to their slavery, and the Armoricans in general to surrender their freedom, to recognise the Emperor as their rightful ruler, and to begin once again to pay the crushing Imperial taxes on the understanding that there would be no reprisals? But that would have been tantamount to surrender and would hardly have appealed to the victorious rebels even without reprisals. It is not at all easy to see on what terms the Emperor was to 'pardon' Tibatto and his men. On the other hand, it is noteworthy that it was the rebels who at first tried to reach an accommodation with the Emperor. It was they, not he, who made overtures to the bishop of Auxerre, so as to persuade him to intervene. At the time when these overtures were made, then, the rebels may have had some doubts about their chances of ultimate victory, doubts which they eventually, and unwisely, discarded.

The entire Armorican incident began, as far as Germanus was concerned, when a delegation of Armoricans called upon him in Auxerre. We are not told what this delegation wanted the bishop to do. As a result of its request, the bishop hurried off to intercept the column of nomad-horsemen which was

[29] *Ibid.*, §40 (280,3).
[30] *Ibid.*, §28 (272,15); §40 (280,2).
[31] Gallic 'Chronicle of A.D. 452', §117 (ed. Mommsen, *Chronica Minora*, I.660).
[32] Thompson, 'Zosimus', p. 461.

already on its way to Armorica. It is a fair inference that the rebels doubted their capacity to resist this onslaught. At all events, what did the bishop hope to achieve by an interview with Goar? And what did the Armoricans hope that he would achieve for them? It was Goar who proposed a truce in order to see if Germanus could obtain a 'pardon' from the government. Was it the Armorican aim, too, at this stage to be amnestied? Did they (as distinct from Germanus) accept the Alan king's offer? We are not told that the bishop consulted them: were they even interested in an amnesty? If not, we can understand why they resumed the war at a moment which for Germanus could hardly have been more embarrassing. But in that case the purpose of their visit to Germanus at Auxerre is not easy to detect.

Be that as it may, it is clear that there was a distinct difference in the attitudes of Germanus and Constantius towards the Armoricans. Germanus took the utmost trouble to save them from the inevitable atrocities of an Alan invasion. He granted them his *uenia*, his 'pardon', for their revolt (whatever such *uenia* may have amounted to). He travelled all the way to Ravenna to try to save them. He could hardly have done more to help them. He cannot have been wholly unsympathetic to their aims, nobleman though he was. It was he, of all the bishops of Gaul, whom the Armoricans sought out. But in Constantius's language there is no hint of sympathy with them. We have seen how he dismisses them as insolent, fickle, and so on, and their leader Tibatto as a man of perfidy.

IX

CONSTANTIUS

Constantius used to be described as a priest of Lyon. Now, he may have been a cleric, but there is no evidence to show his rank, and we cannot be at all sure that he was a priest.[1] Why do we speak of him as being 'of Lyon'? Two matters connect him with that city. It was Patiens, bishop of Lyon, who incited him to write the *Vita* of Germanus; and Constantius with Sidonius Apollinaris, who was probably a native of Lyon, and one Secundinus, whose birthplace is unknown, composed verses to be inscribed on the walls of a church which Patiens dedicated in the city.[2] Perhaps these two achievements, his *Vita* and his verses, are enough to place him in Lyon.

But, if so, the role which Lyon plays in his narrative is unexpected. In the mid-430s Germanus travelled from Auxerre to Arles in order to interview the Praetorian Prefect there. Constantius gives a detailed description of Germanus's stay at Alesia (Alise-Sainte-Reine, dép. Côte d'Or), where the priest, Senator, was an old friend of his and a nobleman.[3] The priest's wife was called Nectariola. Germanus indirectly worked a miracle on an acquaintance of theirs, a certain Agrestius *bene ingenuus*.[4] So we learn the names and relationships of three persons living at Alesia, all of them well-to-do. When we arrive at Arles we are introduced to Hilary, the bishop who aspired to be an autocrat (although Constantius does not mention any such ambition),[5] Auxiliaris the Prefect and his wife (whose name is not given). But between Alesia and Arles the saint visited Lyon; and since Lyon appears to have been Constantius's home-town, we might have hoped to learn the names and relationships of a very considerable number of its inhabitants. In his own native place we might have expected Constantius to have had access to a more than ordinary number of traditions and recollections about the saint, and detailed reports by and about the persons who had met him and whom

---

[1] Levison, *apud* Krusch & Levison, *Passiones*, VII.230, n. 8.

[2] Sidonius, *Epistulae*, II.10,2f.

[3] *Vita*, §22 (267,5). For another Gallic cleric called Senator who is known from 456 see the report in *Année épigraphique* (1928) 85, with Marrou, 'Le dossier', p. 340. Duchesne, *Fastes*, II.163, lists a 'Senator' as bishop of Lyon in the middle of the fifth century. Of course, the most famous bearer of the name was Cassiodorus.

[4] *Vita*, §22 (267,12). For *ingenuus* thus see *Thesaurus Linguae Latinae*, VI.1545, line 50.

[5] For bibliography on Hilary see Mathisen, 'Hilarius', and the references in his footnotes, and especially Kolon, *Die Vita*.

he had cured by his miraculous powers, and in general what he had said and done. But the fact is very different. Constantius reports practically nothing about the visit to Lyon. The contrast with his accounts of what happened at Alesia and at Arles is sharp. In a mere five lines he gives us a small crop of platitudes, telling how enormous crowds had welcomed the saint who had blessed them, cured infirmities with his blessing, and had left in a hurry, *licet festinus abscesserit*.[6] He does not refer to the local bishop or tell us what *he* thought of the distinguished visitor. He does not refer to his own relatives: did *they* have no dealings with Germanus? Not a single person is named in this flat, meagre account. It is hard to see why the chapter relating to Lyon of all places, the writer's native city (according to the common view), should be so thin and empty compared with the chapters on either side of it which take the saint to Alesia and Arles. There is a problem here which is not easy to resolve. Can it be that in the years 480–90, when Constantius was collecting his information, the visit was forgotten, having been nothing very much out of the ordinary? Can it be that the presence of Germanus in the great city was a detail to which nobody had paid much attention?

The fact is that it is difficult to study the life of St Germanus of Auxerre in detail without feeling a growing distrust of the *Vita* by Constantius – not perhaps of the whole of it, but of substantial parts. At a first reading we think that, in spite of its reticences when dealing with the saint's activities in Britain, yet on the whole it is internally consistent; that, by and large, its story is not improbable, at any rate in outline; and that it does not flatly contradict our other sources, such as they are. But when we look at the matter a little more closely, doubts begin to daunt us. It *does* contradict such other pieces of information as we possess, and it also contains internal obscurities.

According to Constantius, a 'widely attended synod' (*numerosa synodus*)[7] of Gallic bishops unanimously begged Germanus and Lupus to travel to Britain. No such synod is known from any other source, and Hugh Williams expressed the opinion of many when he wrote that 'The very fact that this Council is said to be *numerosa*, while no other record of it has survived, is suspicious; and I am unable fully to believe that it was ever held; it seems to be the creation of Constantius'.[8] On the occasion of the second visit Constantius is more vague: Germanus was urged by the 'prayers of all the bishops' (*preces sacerdotum omnium*),[9] that is to say, of all the Gallic bishops. Is that likely? *All* of them? But for the first visit we have an alternative version. According to Prosper,[10] the circumstances were entirely different. He has nothing to say of a Gallic synod. He tells us that Pope Celestine, at the instigation of the deacon Palladius, sent Germanus to Britain as his own

[6] *Vita*, §23 (268,1–5).
[7] *Ibid.*, §12 (259,8).
[8] Williams, *Christianity*, p. 224. I do not know why Chadwick, *Poetry and Letters*, p. 257f., speaks of it as a 'Synod of Arles'; cf. Benoit, 'L'hilarianum', p. 182, 'à Troyes ou à Arles'.
[9] *Vita*, §25 (269,15).
[10] §1301 (ed. Mommsen, *Chronica Minora*, I.472).

representative. Scholars have tried to combine this version of what happened with what Constantius tells us: Celestine recommended Germanus to the Gallic synod, or perhaps Germanus was selected by the bishops and then his journey was sanctioned and confirmed by the Pope, or perhaps Germanus went as the representative of Pope Celestine whereas Lupus went as the envoy of the Gallic Church, or maybe the Britons appealed first to the Continental Church and ultimately to Pope Celestine, although it may be that Constantius is welding together two traditions, one from Auxerre, the other from Troyes, and so on. But, as Levison pointed out, whoever weighs the sources will reject such attempts at reconciliation. Prosper wrote only four years after the event and had every reason to report the truth. Constantius wrote fifty or sixty years after the event and might well have been unaware of who exactly had initiated the journey. Hence he might well have *assumed* that a Gallic synod must have done so. But it is difficult to see how a Gallic synod could have had the authority to send one of its number to Britain as the papal 'vicar' or 'representative'; and if we accept those words of Prosper, *uice sua*, meaning 'vicar', the initiative can have come only from the pope. In fact, the only safe course is to accept what Prosper tells us. In addition, we may, if we wish, suppose that a Gallic synod was perhaps involved in some unidentifiable way, or more probably that a number of Gallic bishops were sounded out informally and – not meeting in a formal synod – encouraged Germanus to go.[11]

What is most disturbing in all this is that Constantius appears to know nothing whatever about the involvement of the pope. According to him, the whole matter was a local Gallic affair in which Rome was not concerned. But, if he had been aware of it, could Constantius possibly have omitted the interest of the pope as a mere detail not worth mentioning? It seems impossible; and I am inclined to suppose that he had never heard of Celestine's discussions with Palladius. And yet, to make the matter even more baffling, it seems clear that Palladius was a deacon of the church of Auxerre, not of the church of Rome.[12]

But if we doubt Constantius's version of the appointment of Germanus and Lupus, we also doubt *eo ipso* the existence of the delegation of Britons who allegedly travelled to Gaul to ask for help against the heretics. And so we could quickly be reduced to guesswork in trying to answer the question how the pope knew that the faith in Britain was in danger. It might well have been the case (we could guess) that Palladius, on a visit to Britain for the same or another purpose, had come to the conclusion that the position of the orthodox faith there was imperilled and that action ought to be taken. Then, as Prosper informs us, he incited the pope to act. I have assumed[13] the

<hr />

[11] Levison, 'Bischof Germanus', p. 121f. See also Levison, *apud* Krusch & Levison, *Passiones*, VII.227, n. 5, and 231 *ad fin*.

[12] See Hanson, *Saint Patrick*, pp. 52–4.

[13] See p. 7 above.

existence of some kind of orthodox organisation in Britain which invited the Gallic bishops to come over and which arranged the debate with the Pelagians. Even if we accept Prosper's version, we must assume the existence of such a British organisation to arrange the debate – it was not arranged by Germanus himself, nor is he likely to have crossed the sea to Britain without being wholly certain that he would be able to meet the Pelagians and debate with them. But what incited Palladius to act in 429? It may be that he had heard of some dramatic development – say, the conversion of the bishop of London to the heresy along with many of his clergy (although we must not make too much of the absence of any British bishops from the great debate: there was no bishop in evidence, as we have seen, when Germanus reached Lyon a few years later). On any reckoning, if we admit the authority of Prosper, it would seem to be the case that Palladius was in close touch with Britain in and before 429. And if we agree that Palladius was in close touch with Britain in 429 and may have visited that island, it is not a big step to go on to suppose that it was he who, first of all Continental clerics, noticed the need for a bishop to be sent to the christians in Ireland, the post to which he was himself appointed in 431.

It seems doubtful whether Constantius had any knowledge of the specific British context in which Germanus paid his first visit. Had Constantius ever heard of Agricola? He certainly was aware that the Pelagians were winning striking victories in Britain, but had he any exact information, say, about the identity of the leading Pelagians in the island and whether they were Britons by birth or exiles from the Continent? Did he know in what area or areas of Britain they won their successes, or how widespread these successes had been in any one region? Did he know what inroads Pelagianism had made into the British clergy? Did he even know what crisis had arisen which could be countered only by a visit of eminent Gallic bishops? It is hardly open to doubt that Prosper was well informed on all or most of these matters: was Constantius well informed on *any* of them? He represents the British delegation in Gaul as saying that Pelagianism had 'seized upon the peoples far and wide', *late populos occupasse.*[14] Yet, when he brings Germanus and Lupus to Britain, he takes them only from the coast where they landed to the scene of the debate, then on a flying visit to Verulamium, and finally back again to the coast. It can hardly be said that they journeyed 'far and wide' to defeat the enemy. In view of that word *late*, we might have expected that the saint would have travelled to several major centres of population to refute the heretics instead of going to one only. We might have expected him to bring the heretics to debate not once only but several times. Yet even when he reached Verulamium, according to Constantius's own view, his work of propaganda was clearly over: he did not debate with any heretics there, and indeed there is no hint that there were any Pelagians in the vicinity of St Alban's tomb. Nor is he reported to have debated with Pelagians after

[14] *Vita.* § 12 (259,6).

leaving Verulamium. He went, or intended to go, straight home. It is by no means out of the question that Constantius has misrepresented the Britons' message to Gaul when he makes them say that the heresy had won victories *late*, 'over a large area'. I think it to be likely that the heretics' victory had been won in a single but crucially important centre, and that if the Pelagians were to win there permanently the consequences of their victory might be catastrophic, whereas if they were defeated in that one place they were instantly defeated in Britain as a whole.

Some may think that Constantius could not have answered any of the questions set out in the preceding paragraph. He did not know that the pope had been personally involved in the situation in Britain – otherwise he could not possibly have omitted to say so.[15] Hence his narrative about the antecedents of the first expedition to Britain is largely guesswork on his part: it is what Constantius thought had in all probability happened. His narrative about the exploits of Germanus and Lupus in Britain is so impressionistic that I strongly doubt whether he had ever questioned Lupus of Troyes about them. After all, Lupus had been bishop in or before 429, when he would probably have been over thirty years of age. In 478/9, then, if he was still alive (as he is usually thought to have been)[16] he was an exceedingly old man, and when Constantius was collecting his information about Germanus this Lupus, if he was still alive and if Constantius in fact questioned him, may well have been able to remember very little. But one matter he could hardly have forgotten even if he were a hundred years old. He could not have forgotten that it was the pope himself who had sanctioned his mission. If he had forgotten this, he must indeed have been in an advanced stage of senility. I infer that Constantius did not question Lupus either because the old man was too old to remember anything at all or because he was already dead when Constantius began to collect his information or simply – although this is unlikely – because he did not know him. What we can be certain of is that Constantius did indeed make efforts – on the whole, outstandingly successful efforts – to find out the facts of Germanus's career on the Continent. He was far from young himself at the time in question; Bardy[17] estimates that Constantius was at least sixty towards the year 473, when Sidonius[18] describes him as *persona aetate grauis infirmitate fragilis*.

No doubt others besides Lupus had accompanied Germanus to Britain; but half a century is a long time, and by 475–90 – the period in which Constantius was working – most of them, perhaps all of them, were already

---

[15] On the other hand, it must be conceded that Sidonius never once in the whole corpus of his works mentions the pope of Rome: this remarkable fact was pointed out by Hanson, 'The Church', p. 3.

[16] But note the doubts of Krusch, *Passiones*, III.118; cf. Krusch & Levison, *Passiones*, VII.284f.; Stevens, *Sidonius*, p. 206; Chadwick, *Poetry and Letters*, p. 258. For an account in English of this Lupus see Chadwick, *ibid.*, pp. 275–85.

[17] Bardy, 'Constance', p. 94.

[18] Sidonius, *Epistulae*, III.2,3.

in their graves. Many of them had doubtless been lying there for years. What Constantius could draw upon, then, was not first-hand but second-hand or even third-hand information. His informants could only report what they had heard – perhaps many years ago – from the priest X or the deacon Y who long ago had sailed with the two bishops to Britain. For Germanus's activities in Gaul and Italy a larger number of informants would have been available. Indeed, Constantius seems to mention some of his authorities for Italian affairs. He remarks that six venerable bishops attended on Germanus in Ravenna, and he goes on to say that these testified to his works for many years, *hi testes operum suorum* [sic] *multis fuere temporibus*.[19] But he speaks of them in the past tense, and Bardy[20] is inclined to think that they were themselves dead by the time when Constantius was collecting his information and that their reports, too, were known to him only at second hand. This is probably right, but their reports *were*, I fancy, in some sense known to him.

It may be that the problem is rather to explain the extreme detail and accuracy of the narrative of events in Gaul and Italy than to account for the indefinite character of the British narrative. To assemble by verbal enquiry small details of what had happened half a century ago is no easy task. But Constantius was successful – with some exceptions – in the case of Germanus's actions in Gaul and Italy. The term 'successful', however, is a relative one, and it cannot be denied that he can hardly ever report Germanus's words in direct speech or even claim to summarise the speeches and sermons of his hero. Again, he tells us that Germanus had practised as an advocate in the court of the Urban or Praetorian Prefect.[21] Having raised the matter, why does he not specify the prefect in question? Gaudemet remarks that Constantius was either indifferent to the saint's career before he became bishop or simply did not know and evidently could not find out details about it, although it is also possible that he did not think it important to try to find out.[22] The fact is that Constantius has little information at his disposal about Germanus's career as bishop before 429, that is, before the first visit to Britain. Apart from some unlocalised and indefinite miracles, he has only one personal name and one specific achievement to report, and this is the incident of Ianuarius, *princeps praesidalis officii*.[23] Yet at this date Germanus must have been a very prominent bishop: otherwise, he would hardly have been chosen for the British mission in 429. Moreover, it is odd that one so meticulous in his use of technical language should leave us in the dark about the provincial governorship (if that is what it was) which Germanus was holding when he was appointed bishop. He is usually taken to have been *dux* of that huge area of Gaul known as the *tractus Armoricanus et Neruicanus*. That is

---

[19] *Vita*, §37 (277,25); cf. §43 (281,16).
[20] Bardy, 'Constance', p. 106.
[21] See p. 10 above.
[22] Gaudemet, 'La carrière', p. 111f.
[23] *Vita*, §7 (254,10).

likely, although there is no certainty.[24] And even after 429, although the story takes Germanus to Lyon,[25] Constantius says not a word about his relations with the bishop there. Did the local bishop – his identity at this date appears to be unknown – ignore him, or was no information available?

The account of the second visit to Britain is an altogether different matter. It is an extreme example of his lack of success. For this journey it is clear that Constantius could find no worthwhile informant at all. Apart from the alleged miracle of the cure of Elafius's lame son, Constantius knows practically nothing about this expedition. Germanus was accompanied by Severus, whose see Constantius apparently did not know; he preached successfully to the people, and some of the heretics were exiled. We have already seen[26] that this last matter may well be a mistake and that the event may have taken place during the first, not the second, visit, although it is not out of the question that Pelagians were exiled on both occasions. It would certainly be a mistake to infer, as has been inferred, from the brevity of Constantius's account of the second visit that 'the second victory of St Germanus was incomparably easier than the first'.[27] It may have been harder. And it would be equally rash to suppose, as has been supposed, that Germanus won no victory over the barbarians on his second visit because, no doubt, the Britons were leading a less threatened life than in 429.[28] It may have been very much *more* threatened. In our dealings with the second visit to Britain an argument based on silence would be so dangerous as to be worthless. Hanson was right:[29] 'It may be doubted if Constantius knew anything about this second visit, except that it took place'. But, as we have seen,[30] it is this account which leaves us with the problem of the name 'Elafius'.

Constantius makes one extraordinary judgment on Britain as it was at the time when he was writing (probably in the decade 480–90). Since the success of Germanus's second visit to Britain, he says, the faith in those parts remains unimpaired 'to this day', 'even now', *etiam nunc*.[31] Hoare[32] remarks that 'by the time that Constantius wrote, heathen Teutons had overrun the eastern half of the island'. And so he concludes that the faith remained intact 'in western Britain, where these events had probably taken place'. But it was argued above[33] that on both occasions Germanus visited one and the same

---

[24] For Germanus's earlier career see especially Gaudemet, 'La carrière', pp. 111–18. Borius, *Constance*, pp. 65, 69, 74, surprisingly more than once calls Germanus *defensor ciuitatis* as if he did not know that this is a technical term for a municipal official whose task was to act as judge in minor cases. It was far beneath a man of Germanus's standing.

[25] See p. 78 above.

[26] See p. 29 above.

[27] So de Plinval, 'Les campagnes', p. 148; cf. Borius, *Constance*, p. 87.

[28] So Demougeot, 'Les invasions', p. 44.

[29] See p. 4 above.

[30] *Ibid.*

[31] *Vita*, § 27 (271,2).

[32] *The Western Fathers*, p. 308, n. 1.

[33] See p. 47 above.

part of Britain. Now, it is almost impossible to believe that the first visit brought the saint to western Britain, for few will hold that a joint raiding party of Picts and Saxons made its appearance off the west coast or even the southwestern coast of Britain. As far as our evidence goes, the main thrust of the raids of the Picts seems always to have fallen on the richer eastern coast (though perhaps not the most northerly part of it, which would have been less profitable to plunderers than the lands lying somewhat farther south); and a raid by Saxons on the west coast is out of the question. That is to say, Germanus must have come to eastern Britain on both occasions, and Constantius's claim for the survival of orthodox christianity *ca* 480 calls for some comment.

To be sure, there were isolated pockets of Romano-British christianity which survived throughout the most terrible days of the Anglo-Saxon invasions.[34] But they are not what Constantius has in mind. He distinctly implies that the part of Britain which his hero visited remained Catholic as a whole (in so far, presumably, as it had been christian at all) and was not menaced by the heretics (still less obliterated by pagans). At the risk of drowning the reader in boredom, I should repeat that Constantius is a hagiographer, not an historian. He makes this assertion about the survival of Catholicism not in order to bring his readers up to date on the subject of British christianity but in order to glorify Germanus. He is not thinking of the conflict between christianity and paganism. His theme here is the conflict between Catholicism and Pelagianism, and what he is telling us is that 'in that region even today the faith remains unimpaired', *ut in illis locis etiam nunc fides intemerata perduret*.[35] Pelagianism had been defeated there permanently. Germanus had won a lasting success. Some forty years after his visit orthodoxy was triumphant. Even now heresy is no problem in the area which Germanus visited.

As a eulogy of Germanus these assertions are legitimate by the standards of the hagiographers. As a description of southeastern Britain in the decade 480–90 they are in all probability a travesty of the truth. The salient fact about the area which Germanus had visited was not the failure of Pelagianism to come to life again but the near destruction of christianity itself there. In my view, Constantius was able to misrepresent the facts so radically because neither he nor his readers knew anything at all about the true condition of southeastern Britain in their own day: communications had long since been broken off to an extent which made it all but impossible for the general public of educated men in Gaul to learn what exactly was going on there. Were Constantius's readers so ill informed about British conditions as to accept what he told them? It looks as though that were the case. If they had been well informed Constantius might have exposed himself to ridicule. Their

[34] See Cameron, 'Eccles'.
[35] *Vita*, §27 (271,2).

knowledge was so cloudy that they would accept his points without losing faith in him altogether. Indeed, if they knew anything of Britain they would also have queried his description of the island as 'very wealthy', *opulentissima insula*,[36] relating to 429. Perhaps it had been a legitimate epithet at that date – although it might be more apposite when used of Milan,[37] not yet devastated by Attila – but the reason for which Constantius uses it about Britain is no doubt to show that the land which Germanus restored to orthodoxy was no mere remote, poverty-stricken island on the far side of the Ocean, but a rich and prosperous place which it was important to rescue from heresy. Germanus had not wasted his time.

Needless to say, there is no question of Constantius deliberately misleading his readers in this connexion. He knew no more than they did. And his purpose was not to write a report on contemporary Britain. His purpose was to glorify St Germanus. It is not surprising that Constantius can tell us little about Britain in Germanus's time, for he knew little about it as it was then. He had few sources of information. Now it appears that he and his readers knew little about it as it was in 480–90. Communications even with the south-east of the island – perhaps we ought to say, *especially* with the south-east – had long since been cut. What is certain is that it would be unwise to erect great theories about the survival of christianity in Britain on the basis of that phrase *etiam nunc*.[38] The most which we can reasonably infer is that Constantius thought heresy to be no problem in those places where christianity still survived; but even he probably did not know where those places were located.

We have seen that at the end of his book Constantius apologises for (among other things) omitting much of what he knew about the deeds of Germanus.[39] This was a commonplace among the writers of the lives of saints.[40] We have already discussed his omissions in connexion with Armorican events. He also leaves us in ignorance about the nature of the services to the Church in Gaul which brought Germanus his great renown before 429. When Sidonius, later on, wishes to praise to the utmost Annianus, bishop of Orléans, he says that he was the equal of Lupus and not unequal to Germanus. When Reverentius, author of the *Vita S. Hilarii Arelatensis*, writing about the year 500, wishes to bolster up the correctness of Hilary's attack on Celidonius of Besançon, he associates Germanus with his hero's action, thereby hoping to make it seem respectable.[41] Why do these men speak in such respectful terms? Wherein lay Germanus's greatness? We do not know. The surprising fact is that Constantius fails to explain it to us. He makes no

---

[36] *Ibid.*, § 18 (265,7).
[37] *Ibid.*, § 33 (275,6).
[38] *Ibid.*, § 27 (271,2).
[39] *Ibid.*, § 46 (283,5). See p. 73, n. 13, above.
[40] Bardy, 'Constance', p. 100.
[41] Sidonius, *Epistulae*, VIII.15,1; *Vita S. Hilarii Arelatensis*, § 16. It looks as though the author of this *Vita* knew little or nothing about Germanus except his enormous respectability. On this *Vita* see Kolon, *Die Vita*.

reference to the character of Germanus's conversation or of his sermons. He mentions no writings of his, neither homilies nor letters nor anything else. Yet even the meagre Gallic 'Chronicle of A.D. 452' gives him an entry to mark his *floruit* (*s.a.* 433), and says that he was famous because of his virtues (or miracles) and the rigour of his life.[42] Wherever he went in Gaul, Italy, and even Britain, crowds came out to see and hear him. Why? What had made his name so well known? The only inference which we can draw from what Constantius tells us is that his fame was due simply to the ferocious way in which he mortified the flesh. He imposed upon himself so many 'crosses', according to his biographer (if this is the right term to use of a hagiographer), that he dragged out his life in one prolonged martyrdom.[43]

Unfortunately from his own point of view, Constantius in an unguarded moment tells an anecdote about Germanus's arrival in Milan which might be taken to mean that the Italians had no idea whatever of his identity.[44] But that is beside the point. It is an oversight.

The most remarkable pieces of information given by Constantius about Germanus's life in Gaul relate to the saint's activities in the cities, not in the countryside. True, when he deals with the period of Germanus's bishopric which fell before 429, a period on which he is remarkably ill informed, he describes two miracles which the saint performed while on a journey.[45] (We do not learn where he was going to or from on this journey.) One of these miracles amounted simply to burying properly the bodies of two criminals improperly buried before. The miracle consisted of his finding the bodies in the first place through the assistance of a ghost. On the same journey (*in eodem itinere*) he lodged with some *mediocres personae*[46] – being mere *mediocres* they did not need to be named – and noticed that at daybreak the local cocks did not crow. It turned out that they had not crowed for a long time past. Germanus paid for his lodging by restoring to the cocks their vocal powers, which they exercised thenceforward to the point of driving the inhabitants almost to distraction, *usque ad molestiam*.[47] These are inferior miracles, as miracles go. They would do little credit to any self-respecting mediaeval saint. If Germanus's fame had depended on exploits such as these, Constantius would have had little temptation to write an account of him. Further, on his journey to interview the Prefect Auxiliaris at Arles, when he was still inside the *territorium* of Auxerre, his horse was stolen. The thief repented and restored the horse, pleading that no other course was open to him since the horse refused to go forward any

---

[42] Mommsen, *Chronica Minora*, I.660: 'Germanus episcopus Altisiodori uirtutibus et uitae districtione clarescit'. There is an inadequate article on *districtio* in the *Thesaurus Linguae Latinae*, V.1550, line 12. The Gallic Chronicle is not cited in it, nor the *Vita Abbatum Acaunensium*, § 9 (edd. Krusch & Levison, *Passiones*, VII.335, line 10). Nor does the *Thesaurus* quote the meaning 'rigour', 'severity'.

[43] *Vita*, § 4 (253,13).

[44] *Ibid.*, § 32 (274,21).

[45] *Ibid.*, § § 10–11 (257,7–259,4).

[46] *Ibid.*, § 11 (258,20f.).

[47] *Ibid.* (259,3).

farther.[48] By the standards of mediaeval miracle-workers, Germanus (if we were to judge him by this example of his craft) would be classified as a hopeless failure, a duffer of 'C3' quality. Indeed, some may think that when Constantius uses such a phrase as *sanabantur infirmi*,[49] without any detail whatever, we can infer that he had no specific information and merely threw in these phrases for effect as a matter of routine: they do not even prove that sick persons were cured. On his final journey to Italy he revisited his old friend, the priest Senator, and cured a dumb girl aged twenty years.[50] (It is not clear why Constantius thinks it important to tell us her age.) When he was passing through the *territorium* of Autun,[51] he cured the hand of an unnamed girl of marriageable age whose fingers were bent rigidly and permanently into her palm with distressing results as her fingernails grew. After leaving Milan he was asked to turn aside off the road to Ravenna in order to visit the estate of Leporius, *uir spectabilis* (the second highest grade of the nobility), for no less a fee than 200 *solidi*.[52] He cured those who were ill – Constantius makes no great or indeed specific claims – and resumed his journey to the court. This last incident, the visit to Leporius, reflects not so much the powers of Germanus as a miracle-worker as the fact that the high nobility sought him out and were glad to entertain him in their homes – or, at any rate, that *one* of them was glad to do so.

Of these five 'miracles', if they deserve the name, which Germanus is said to have worked in the countryside of Gaul and Italy, only one entails naming the person who benefited from the work – Leporius, *uir spectabilis*. The others concern persons who were of low degree and hence were not worth naming. In all of them the bishop is on a journey: we never hear of his performing a miracle while making his ordinary rounds of his diocese. He is never reported to have preached to the rustics of his diocese. In fact, Germanus's career was essentially an urban one.

It is unfortunate that those passages of the *Vita* which take Germanus into the countryside do not make it entirely clear whether the countryfolk of Gaul were in the main christian or pagan at this date. We have seen[53] that the saint founded his monastery on the other side of the River Yonne from Auxerre so as to help bring the people to the Catholic faith.[54] Otherwise, except where he speaks of the savage King Goar, Constantius never refers to paganism. Were it not for the reason for which he founded his monastery, we might conclude that paganism was no longer a problem in the vicinity of Auxerre or along the roads which Germanus travelled. But in the stories of the haunted house, the cocks which could not crow (§§ 10–11), the theft of his horse (§ 20), and the other incidents which happened in the countryside, the

[48] *Ibid.*, § 22 (266,17).
[49] *Ibid.*, § 37 (277,22); cf. § 34 (276,1).
[50] *Ibid.*, § 29 (272,21).
[51] *Ibid.*, § 30 (273,14).
[52] *Ibid.*, § 33 (275,22).
[53] See p. 16 above.
[54] *Vita*, § 6 (254,4).

actors are never said to have been either pagan or christian. It is true that more than once great crowds turned up to catch sight of the saint,[55] but they are not said to have been moved to do so by the christian faith or to have been inspired to more earnest belief by what they saw. And when Constantius says that on all the roads[56] where Germanus prayed or taught while travelling from Auxerre to Autun, oratories and crosses stand 'to this day' (*in hodiernum diem*),[57] we can infer no more than that some members of the crowds were enthusiastic christians.

One reason why Constantius does not linger to tell us the sentiments of these crowds is that they were for the most part composed of the poor, still Celtic-speakers (it seems) for the most part, all of them rustics and all of them therefore equally unimportant – so unimportant that their names would be of no possible interest to him or his readers. All the persons whose names he does report were townsfolk and more or less rich. The exception is one which proves the rule: he does name one country-dweller, the rich estate- and slave-owner Leporius who was able to pay him no less a fee than two hundred *solidi*. (Bear in mind that a man could live, or at any rate exist, on two *solidi* a year, or even less.[58]) Germanus himself, of course, was *parentibus splendidissimis procreatus*,[59] though not a nobleman: he was not a member of the clarissimate, still less a *uir spectabilis* like Leporius. And Constantius, too, was of noble birth, as Sidonius tells us[60] (*nobilitate sublimis*). We must not forget that Constantius is a nobleman writing for the educated, literate minority, a tiny minority, the propertied class of town and villa. In essence, he is also writing about such people. He is describing the life of the rich or relatively rich – the landowners, public servants, the higher clergy – who could travel peaceably through Gaul and visit Italy or Britain, and write and read books. The rustic poor do indeed figure in the narrative, but they are a homogeneous, undifferentiated, nameless mass. They gather in crowds around the great man. They benefit from his wonderworking. They have no initiative. They are acted upon: they do not act. His readers were not interested in them as individuals. That is why he does not analyse the motives of the Armoricans in 435–7. His readers were indeed interested in the action taken by the government to suppress them but not at all in their reasons for dispossessing the landowners, abolishing the use of Roman law, and so on.

But there is one exception. There is one man of the people who is not anonymous. Tibatto forced himself upon the notice of Germanus and Constantius and the Chronicler of A.D. 452 and even upon the notice of Aetius and of Valentinian III himself. His aim was to secede from the Roman empire, and although he failed now his cause triumphed a few years

[55] *Ibid.*, §21 (267,1) and §30 (273,12 & 15).
[56] *Ibid.*, §30 (273,12), *per omnes aggeres*, is not 'every eminence', as Hoare, *The Western Fathers*, p. 310, renders it, but 'along all the highways'.
[57] *Vita*, §30 (273,13).
[58] Jones, *The Later Roman Empire*, I.447.
[59] *Vita*, §1 (251,3).
[60] *Epistulae*, III.2,3.

later.[61] We can hardly doubt that he was inspired to act as he did by the success of the Britons in 409.[62] Germanus was not without sympathy, or at any rate understanding, for the Armoricans of Tibatto. He did his utmost to help them. Constantius does not tell us why. The answer would hardly have reflected credit on his hero in the eyes of those who were likely to read his book.

---

[61] Thompson. 'Procopius', p. 503.
[62] See p. 36 above.

X

AFTER GERMANUS

We cannot even begin to reconstruct the course of the Saxon conquest of Britain from the evidence of the literary sources alone. The only detailed evidence available to us is that of archaeology and of the place-names. But the Latin authors do enable us to state some general factors, although these relate only to the fifth century and only to eastern England.[1]

Once the Saxons were settled on the land in England social development was rapid. It is difficult, therefore, to argue back from later times, that is, to try to deduce the institutions of the fifth century from what we know of the seventh and later centuries. Between the age of St Germanus of Auxerre and that of St Augustine of Canterbury Saxon society had been revolutionised. What had been groupings of kindreds and retinues in Germanus's day were now overlaid by a series of comparatively highly developed states in the seventh century, with kings who could not only publish but also enforce codes of law. The fifth-century warbands could not have exploited a subject population or administered a Roman landed estate. The kings could do both. The differences, in fact, were so fundamental that to try now to deduce from the later period what 'must' have been the institutions of the earlier is a mistake in method. In other words, the only Latin sources upon which we can legitimately draw are those which date from the fifth century itself (together, it must be said, with Gildas and Bede).

On the date of the 'Arrival' of the Saxons Bede appears to have been the victim of his own learning: he knew not one but two accounts of what he took to be this event, and he does not seem to have distinguished them clearly, one from the other. He refers three times to the incident which Gildas reports, the settlement as Federates[2] in northeastern Britain of three shiploads of Saxons together with some later arrivals. I am inclined to think that this event took place *ca* 460, but Bede dated it to the joint reign of Valentinian III and Marcian, 450–5, and only a brave man would say that he was wrong. But Bede seems to have confused this event with a different one, an event which has been otherwise reported to us only by the Gallic 'Chronicler of A.D. 452'. In fact, this second event is wholly unconnected with the story of Gildas. In a corrupt passage of his chronicle the author writes: 'the British provinces, up to this time [the victims of] various disasters and adversities, were brought under the sway of the Saxons'. To this entry Mommsen assigned the date

---

[1] Jackson, *Language and History*, p. 221f.
[2] For 'Federates' as a technical term, see Jones, *The Later Roman Empire*, II.612.

441/2, but a recent writer has perhaps unnecessarily put it in 445/6.[3] It is to this event that Bede's words seem to refer on the occasions when he is not drawing on Gildas and when he is not referring to Gildas's proud tyrant. He does not claim ever to have given it an exact date. On each of the three occasions on which he refers to it he uses the word 'about', 'approximately' (*circiter*) so many years; and yet he usually gives a fairly precise date and not a round number of years. Admittedly he puts the arrival of the Saxons 'about (*circiter*) 150 years' before Gregory the Great sent out his mission to Britain in 596, viz 446.[4] But later[5] he dates the 'Arrival' 285 years approximately (*circiter*) before the time when he was writing (in 731), viz 446. And elsewhere he dates the *Aduentus* about (*circiter*) 180 years before the baptism of King Edwin in 627, viz about 447.[6] In these three passages he refers to the year 446/7, and in them he makes no reference to Gildas's story of the proud tyrant and his Saxon Federates. There is no reason for thinking that he hit upon the year 446 because Gildas (in quite a different part of his book) spoke of the Britons' appeal to Aetius which was probably sent in that year. Bede is in fact referring to two different and distinct events, one of which (that derived from Gildas) seems to have taken place in northern Britain and the other in the east or south-east. The 'Arrival' of the Saxons is not to be identified with the settlement of Gildas's Federates. Bede offers much the same date as the 'Chronicle of A.D. 452', and I know of no reason to doubt that he has in mind the same event as the Chronicler, although from what source he derived his knowledge of it we do not know. At any rate, it was an event of cataclysmic importance for that part of Britain of which the Chronicler is speaking; and since the Chronicler seems to have lived in south Gaul, he is in all probability referring to southeastern Britain.[7] The 'Arrival' of the Saxons took place, then, several years earlier than the settlement of Gildas's Federates and occurred in a part of the island about which Gildas gives us no information.

The conclusion would seem to be that in addition to the relatively minor incident reported by Gildas (awesome though it may have been in the locality where it happened) an event of far greater importance occurred *ca* 441–7 and was known in later times, and that the Chronicler and Bede (in the second group of these passages) are alike referring to this. It is reasonable to suppose that this event affected the south, probably the south-east, of Britain, the region which a chronicler living in southern Gaul would be most likely to hear of: Boulogne appears even at this date to have been the normal

---

[3] Miller, 'The last British entry'. For Mommsen's view see his *Chronica Minora*, I.660. Miller suggests that 'regarded historiographically, the date [given by the Chronicler] rests specifically upon Bede, *HE* I.13', but I would put the dependence the other way round or rather would refer it to some lost source or tradition, as there is no proof that this 'Chronicle of A.D. 452' postdates Bede.

[4] Bede, *Historia Ecclesiastica*, I.23 with V.24.

[5] *Ibid.*, V.23.

[6] *Ibid.*, II.14.

[7] For some judicious remarks on this entry in the Chronicle see Myres, 'The Adventus', p. 222.

port of entry from Britain.[8] And this is a region about which Gildas says nothing. The nature of the event is suggested almost explicitly by the language used of it by the Chronicler and by Bede: it was not a massive raid but a massive invasion. It was the work not of raiders but of settlers who overwhelmed the Britons over an extensive area. Only such an event as that could reasonably be described as the 'Arrival' of the Saxons or as causing Britain to fall under the sway of the Saxons. Raiding parties had arrived in plenty before now: they were a commonplace even in 367/8. But the fleets which arrived in 446/7 were something very different from the little squadrons of two or three or five ships which had vexed the shores of Britain hitherto. There now came a dramatic change in the progress and nature of the attack – and the most dramatic change of all would be the change from extensive raiding to massive settlement. Whatever settlements may have been planted in Britain hitherto were of minor importance in comparison with what happened in the mid-forties. As another Gallic chronicle, that of A.D. 511,[9] puts it in one short sentence: 'the British provinces, lost by the Romans, fell under the sway of the Saxons'.

As we have seen,[10] nothing whatever is known of the state of mind of the Saxons at the moment when they decided to settle *en masse* in Britain instead of raiding it. Presumably after several generations of raiding it had become common knowledge in the Saxon villages and farmsteads that Britain was a far richer country than their own waterlogged fields and that the inhabitants made none too valorous warriors. For what it is worth, we may note that that is certainly how the Saxons saw it in later days when they looked back on these events: the decisive factor (they thought then) was the knowledge of 'the worthlessness of the Britons and of the excellence of the land'.[11] This they had learned from decades of heavy raiding. But it is not quite right to speak of 'the growing power' of the barbarians. There is no reason to think, as far as I am aware, that the military methods of the Saxons in St Germanus's day were superior to what they had been, say, in 367 or in the time of Carausius. Their morale may well have been higher; but it was the British defence which had grown weaker rather than the power of the Saxons which had grown stronger. And now overnight, we may think, word spread from settlement to settlement that next spring they would embark not only the warriors but many of the women and children and livestock as well, and instead of coming back with the plunder they would stay on in that rich land for ever. There is no need to suppose that some 'great man' decided that the time had come for raiding to end and for mass settlement to begin, or that a council of elders or a popular assembly sounded out opinion in the villages and debated the ins and outs and the pros and cons. There is no reason to think that any one chieftain or any one council of elders had influence over all

---

[8] See p. 51 above.
[9] Mommsen, *Chronica Minora*, I.661.
[10] See p. 46 above.
[11] *Anglo-Saxon Chronicle*, s.a. 449E, from Bede, *Historia Ecclesiastica*, I.15, 'simul et insulae fertilitas ac segnitia Brittonum'.

the communities. Such an idea as that of migration would materialise over-night out of the air, and on this occasion it spread like a thunderclap along the whole length of the north Germanic coastlands. The part of Britain of which the 'Chronicle of A.D. 452' is most likely to have shown knowledge, that is, beyond a doubt, the South-east, had been the victim of many adversities and disasters in the preceding years; but these were all eclipsed by the impact of the fleets of settlers which arrived in 446/7. It was in this very year that the Britons of whom Gildas speaks appealed for help to Aetius and appealed in vain. But their enemies were the Picts and Irish, and the Saxons were not yet an immediate menace to them, although the proud tyrant quickly brought trouble on his own head and on the heads of his neighbours. In the eastern part of England, then, both north and south in the years 441–60 suffered a catastrophe of the first magnitude. In the South this catastrophe consisted not of small and isolated settlements but of permanent and massive settlement.

The Latin sources do not leave us wholly without information about the nature of the Saxon warbands which attacked Britain in the fifth century, but what they tell us is pitifully slight. The Saxons' social organisation seems to have been less developed than that of any major Germanic people living on or near the Western Imperial frontier. Indeed, as far as we can make out, it had changed but little from the kind of society which Julius Caesar had described as normal among the western Germans five hundred years earlier. The chieftain's powers were so slight as to be invisible to a Roman witness. When Sidonius speaks of a boatload of Saxon pirates off the Gallic coast near Saintes he remarks that every man in it is the captain: they all command and obey.[12] In other words, there was no obvious leader. The idea of command, of coercive power, of *imperium*, had not yet evolved among them. No one had autocratic powers over any of the raiding bands. In this respect nothing at all had changed since Caesar's day. And that is not surprising. Personal power had not yet evolved even among the Visigoths in Alaric's day, for example, or among the Rugi in the time of St Severinus, to mention no others.[13] And yet

---

[12] Sidonius, *Epistulae*, VIII.6,13, '. . . contra Saxonum pandos myoparones, quorum quot remiges uideris, totidem te cernere putes archipiratas: ita simul omnes imperant parent, docent discunt latrocinari'.

[13] Claudian, *Bellum Gothicum*, lines 479–517; *de sexto consulatu Honorii*, lines 242f.; Jordanes, *Getica*, § 147; cf. Sidonius, *Carmina*, VII.452f. For the Rugi see Ennodius, *Vita Epifanii* (ed. von Hartel, p. 361, 25: 'qui parere regibus uix dignantur'). Chadwick, *The Origin*, p. 135f., *et passim*, thought that the Anglo-Saxon peoples were subject to 'kingly government'. But genealogies do not tell us what were the powers wielded by the persons named in them, and it would be particularly dangerous to deduce the conditions of the fifth-century leadership from what we know or can infer of the sixth century. On genealogies see Dumville, 'Kingship'. Indeed, Chadwick, *The Origin*, p. 299 (cf. pp. 153 and 300), seems to assume that kingship was originally almost universal and hence that an autocrat like Maroboduus was merely restoring what had once been the normal state of affairs. Now, Gadd, *Ideas*, p. 33, tells us of some ancient Egyptians who believed that kingship existed on the earth even before mankind made its appearance there! We must not follow those ancient Egyptians in believing this. The king who can impose his will upon his followers is a comparatively late arrival in the history of human society. Stenton, *Anglo-Saxon England*, p. 314, holds that the earliest Saxon invaders were 'deferential to kingship as part of the natural order of the world'. There is no reason to think that this is true of the fifth-century Saxons.

94

at least the fourth-century Visigoths were far more advanced than the contemporary Saxons – for one thing, some of them were literate. The fact that the chieftainship was not yet developed explains, no doubt, why we do not know the name of a single Saxon who lived before the year 500 (unless you can swallow Stallion and Mare, Hengist and Horsa, of whom it can at least be said that they are better authenticated than Adam and Eve and King Arthur).[14] And the Old Saxons, who had remained behind on the Continent when the others sailed off to Britain, had not 'developed' much further even at the time when Bede was writing.[15] Consequently, in negotiations with foreign powers it was the 'people' who acted rather than one or more chieftains.[16]

It is in keeping with the backward stage of the Saxons' social development that when they invaded Gaul in 368 they did not enslave their prisoners but massacred them, as they were to do later on in the fifth century in Britain: they could not use adult male prisoners as slaves, and there was no possibility of holding them to ransom.[17] There is no evidence before the sixth century for Saxons exporting slaves to the Continent.[18] Theirs was a society which had a decidedly limited use for slave-labour. In the earliest days of the invasions an adult male slave would have been little more than another hungry mouth to feed. You cannot or will not enslave adult male prisoners (i) unless the productive techniques of your society are sufficiently high to enable the slave to produce a surplus of value over and above what is required to feed, clothe, and shelter him, and to provide him with his tools and raw materials, and (ii) unless you have a system of full-time guards who can prevent him from escaping. But if his kinsmen live only on the other side of the hill or the wood, there is little hope of preventing his escape, no matter how many guards you have, unless you put him to work in a chain-gang – and a chain-gang in agricultural work implies the existence of large estates, and these the fifth-century Saxons did not have. On the other hand, it was not at all difficult to enslave women with children and to put them to work at spinning, weaving, grinding corn, making pots, fetching wood, water, and so on, as well as to serve as concubines. If we find a Saxon leader bearing a Celtic name, that name proves nothing more than that his mother was a

[14] Perhaps we must exclude from this rejection the personal names which are embedded in various place-names, although I know of no reason for thinking that any of these date back to the fifth century. According to Jones *et al.*, *The Prosopography*, II.791, 'Adouacrius', who occupied Angers *cum Saxonibus* about the year 465, in the account of Gregory of Tours, *Historia Francorum*, II.18, was none other than Odoacer, the first barbarian ruler of Italy. I find this hard to credit; but if in fact the two are identical, then he is the first historical Saxon known to us by name.

[15] Bede, *Historia Ecclesiastica*, V.10.

[16] See the passages collected by Schmidt, *Geschichte*, p. 59, n. 5.

[17] Ammianus Marcellinus, *History*, XXVIII.8,5, quoted on p. 44, n. 27, above; Gildas, *De Excidio*, I.25,1. Contrast the Picts in Ammianus Marcellinus, *History*, XXVII.8,7, 'qui uinctos homines agebant et pecora'. When Sidonius, *Epistulae*, VIII.6,15, speaks of the Saxons' killing one in ten of their prisoners, chosen by lot, he is probably telling of a religious rite rather than their normal practice. On the massacre of prisoners by the more primitive among the Germanic peoples see Thompson, 'Slavery', pp. 21–4 = 195–8.

[18] Pelteret, 'Slave raiding', p. 101f.

Briton: to believe that it indicates by definition peaceful intermarriage between Saxon and Briton would reveal a most amusing innocence on the part of the believer.[19] In fact, the enslavement of men was a very different thing and much rarer than the enslavement of women and children in the earliest days of the invasions.[20]

In spite of their primitive society the Saxons were a major military menace because of their unpredictability, as Ammianus stresses in a vivid passage.[21] Yet it is noteworthy that when the Saxons planned a campaign up the Rhine in 356, their first action was to build ships:[22] evidently, they did not always have a fleet of boats ready to use on their marauding expeditions. Sidonius tells us that their ships were stitched together from leather, and in these they would sail off as far as Armorica, to say nothing of Britain.[23] It is not surprising that they were able to bring few horses with them to Britain when they set about invading the island! Try loading a horse into a curragh!

When a Germanic people decided to launch a raid on the Roman provinces on the Continent their normal practice was for each man to bring enough food with him to enable him to reach the Imperial frontier. It was regarded as illegitimate to plunder those of one's own people who lived between the raiders' homes and the frontier.[24] It is hardly open to doubt that, when the Saxons in the earlier fifth century sailed over the sea to Britain, each ship would have held a very small stock of food for the warriors – only such surplus as each warrior could scrape together from last year's harvest for his own immediate needs. And if they sailed in March or April as those Saxons may have done whom St Germanus encountered, the stock would indeed be a small one. If the voyage from their homelands lasted several weeks, as happened sometimes,[25] the raiders would already be hungry when they landed at last in Britain. The immediate aim, then, of each raiding party was to lay hands with no loss of time on enough food to keep its members alive for the period of the plundering. The only recourse was to begin, as soon as they landed from their boats, to look for food; and the success or failure of their expedition might well depend on whether or not they found a supply in their first week in the island. Only for one group of Saxons, as far as we know, was this problem solved quickly. When the proud tyrant of Gildas settled his

[19] Even Jackson, *Language and History*, pp. 207, 244, 249, infers 'intermarriage' from *inter alia* the fact that British personal names were taken into Anglo-Saxon! The fact that this happened in some 'royal' families alters nothing.

[20] See further p. 114 below.

[21] Ammianus Marcellinus, *History*, XXVIII.2,12, 'nec quisquam aduentum eorum cauere poterat inopinum, non destinata, sed uaria petentium et longinqua, et quocumque uentus duxerat, erumpentum: quam ob causam prae ceteris hostibus Saxones timentur ut repentini'. Cf. Sidonius, *Epistulae*, VIII.6,14, 'inprouisus aggreditur praeuisus elabitur', and the whole passage. But this quality is not mentioned in Zosimus, *History*, III.6,1, who stresses their spirit (*thumos*), strength, and perseverance in battle. Julian, *Oration* I.34d, calls them and the Franks the most warlike peoples around the Rhine and the Western Sea.

[22] Zosimus, *History*, III.6,1.

[23] Sidonius, *Carmina*, VII.369f.

[24] Thompson, *The Early Germans*, p. 140f.

[25] Alcock, *Arthur's Britain*, p. 301.

Federates in the east of the northern part of the island, he provided them with rations, *annonae*.[26] The initial problem which the other invaders faced was thus solved for this group at one stroke. But when new arrivals intended not simply to plunder but to settle permanently we do not know what their procedure was. No doubt later arrivals in some cases might be helped by earlier. At all events, as soon as they landed in Britain they would hurry to the British farms and settlements and granaries like wasps to a pot of jam. We should idealise them if we described the bulk of the first Saxon settlers in Britain as other than starving and desperate men. There is no reason in the world for thinking that they shared out the ownership of the farms with their British occupants. 'Continuity' is out of the question. Bear in mind that if a British farmer and his workmen fled from his farm on Saturday night and a Saxon occupied it on Sunday morning, the breach of 'continuity' would be as definitive and absolute as if a year or ten years elapsed between the flight of the one and the arrival of the other. It is not field-systems and artefacts which make up continuity in this sense, but men and women and their exchange of ideas.

When the early settlers reached the shores of Britain they did not find that masses of Saxons had already been settled in the island by the Imperial authorities. It has often been assumed that the government had made a practice of enlisting Saxon and other Germanic federates and of planting them in or just outside the British cities in the fourth and fifth centuries.[27] Now, it was one thing to settle Marcomanni, Burgundians, Vandals, and Alamanni[28] in Britain in the second, third, and fourth centuries, since at those dates Britain was unlikely to be attacked by masses of Marcomanni, Burgundians, and the rest – and the numbers involved cannot have been large. Again, it was one thing for Theodosius I, by the terms of the treaty of 3 October 382, to settle the Visigoths south of the lower Danube in order to keep the Huns (who were newly arrived north of the river) out of the Balkan provinces, or for the Patrician Constantius to plant the Visigoths on the western seaboard of Gaul between the Gironde and the Loire so as to keep the Armoricans from attacking the rich estates of Aquitanica Secunda.[29] Such occasions were rare. But it would have been a very different matter to settle Saxons or any other Germanic mercenaries in eastern Britain so as to fend off other Saxons. It would have been a naive blunder, a suicidal mistake of which no Roman government could have been guilty: the possibility that defenders and intruders might join hands would have been obvious even to the most obtuse Roman government. There is no reason for thinking that long before the time with which we are concerned some British cities had

---

[26] Gildas, *De Excidio*, I.18,5.
[27] On the alleged evidence from 'Romano-Saxon' pottery see Dickinson, 'British antiquity'; Gillam, 'Romano-Saxon pottery'; Fulford, 'Pottery production'; Roberts, *Romano-Saxon Pottery*, p. 168.
[28] Dio Cassius, LXXII.16; Zosimus, *History*, I.68; Ammianus Marcellinus, *History*, XXIX.4,7.
[29] Thompson, *Romans and Barbarians*, pp. 23–37, 251–5.

settled Saxons inside their walls or even outside them.[30] The only military motive for settling Saxons in Britain was that which moved Gildas's proud tyrant: he imported his Federates so as to fend off Pictish raiders sailing down the east coast – for the Picts as well as the Irish were 'overseas peoples', *gentes transmarinae*,[31] and his experience was one which few would wish to copy. He had no intention whatever of using them to keep out other Saxons. He may have been ill advised, but he was not as ill advised as *that* would imply. And it would be wholly wrong to suppose that the Saxon Shore was so called because the Roman authorities planted Saxons there in order to keep out Saxon pirates: it was called by this name because it was under attack by Saxons.[32] If the archaeological finds show that Germanic soldiers were indeed stationed in or near late Roman towns in Britain, there is one thing about these soldiers which we can be sure of: they were not Saxons. (Indeed, the layman, innocent of all archaeological thought, may wonder whether they were Germanic and may even go so far as to doubt whether they were soldiers.) Those archaeologists who tell us of the presence of Germanic mercenaries in Dorchester (Oxfordshire) or in Winchester or the like, by a uniform lapse of memory forget to tell us the identity of the assailants who threatened Dorchester, Winchester, and the others at that time. If such assailants existed at all, they were probably British – British *coloni*, peasants, slaves, and others; and against these, to be sure, the use of Germanic mercenaries would have been in order.

We have an immense amount of information about the fate of the Continental provinces as the barbarians overran them, but that information does not prepare us for what Gildas tells us of Britain in the middle and in the second half of the fifth century. It does not prepare us, for example, for the intensity and the frequency of the famines caused in Britain by the barbarian invasions and reported by Gildas. True, in the great Alamannic invasions, for example, of eastern Gaul in 354/5 the invaders themselves, although they drove off what livestock they could find, sometimes died of starvation before they could lay their hands on food.[33] No doubt, too, many areas of the Continent starved without any reference being made to their sufferings in our extant sources of information. And it is true, too, that when the Vandals, Alans, and Sueves, after causing a famine in Gaul in 409,[34] first entered Spain in the autumn of that fateful year, the inhabitants ran to the protection of the fortified cities where there followed a famine so fearful that cases of cannibalism were reported.[35] But thereafter Hydatius's *Chronicle*

[30] See Johnson, 'Channel commands', p. 82. We know of only one sub-Roman city in the West which admitted Federates within its walls after the fall of the central power in Ravenna, and its experience was unfortunate: Eugippius, *Vita S. Seuerini*, §§1–2, with Thompson, *Romans and Barbarians*, pp. 118–21.

[31] Gildas, *De Excidio*, I.14.

[32] Hind, 'Litus saxonicum', pp. 317–24.

[33] Ammianus Marcellinus, *History*, XVI.5,17; Thompson, *The Early Germans*, p. 144f.

[34] Gallic 'Chronicle of A.D. 511', *s.a.* 411 (ed. Mommsen, *Chronica Minora*, I.654).

[35] Hydatius, *Chronicle*, §48 (ed. Mommsen, *Chronica Minora*, II.17); Olympiodorus of Thebes, fragment 30.

never mentions famine, although that is not to say, of course, that nobody thereafter starved in Spain. Similarly, there was only one serious famine in Noricum during the thirty years (454–83) covered by Eugippius's *Life* of St Severinus, and that was caused by bad weather, not at all by the enemy.[36] We may suspect, of course, that practically every time a city fell some people starved in the general upset. Salvian tells us that, when Trier fell, the number of casualties continued to grow for some time after the sack. Some persons died of wounds, others of burns received when the city was set on fire, and others from exposure *and from starvation.*[37] It is not easy to know how such calamities could be avoided after a sack. Indeed, starvation might well follow in some cases where the citizens managed to scatter even before the attackers arrived.

Now, Gildas covers only a relatively short period of mid-fifth century British history in detail. Yet he tells us that in Britain as a result of the activities of the Picts and Irish there was a famine shortly before 446 which was so terrible that it caused the Britons to fight one another for such food-supplies as still existed: and fighting for this reason is something which we never hear of elsewhere in western Europe throughout the whole of the fifth century. And not long after that date, 446, the island suffered from another famine, which was still spoken of in Gildas's day almost a century later, so frightful was it.[38] Not long after that, according to Gildas, there broke out another and even worse famine, and, when the Saxon Federates rebelled, yet another.[39] There is nothing like it in the recorded history of the Continental Western provinces throughout the fifth century. If we may trust Gildas – and in this connexion there seems no reason why we should not do so – the disruption of the British economy was more devastating than that of Gaul and Spain.

Another surprise in British as contrasted with Continental history in the fifth century is the frequency of the civil wars fought by the Britons among themselves. I have just mentioned that in famine-conditions the Britons were reduced to fighting each other for food.[40] Now, we do not hear of civil war breaking out for this or any other reason among the Roman provincials outside Britain after the collapse of Roman power in the various parts of the West. In Noricum Ripense Roman rule had disappeared before the time

[36] Eugippius, *Vita S. Seuerini*, § 3.
[37] Salvian, *De Gubernatione Dei*, VI.83.
[38] Gildas, *De Excidio*, I.19,3f., 'nam et ipsos mutuo, perexigui uictus breui sustentaculo miserrimorum ciuium, latrocinando temperabant: et augebantur externae clades domesticis motibus, quod huiuscemodi tam crebris direptionibus uacuaretur omnis regio cibi baculo, excepto uenatoriae artis solacio'; I.20,2, 'interea famis dira ac famosissima uagis et nutabundis haeret, quae multos eorum cruentis compulit praedonibus sine dilatione uictas dare manus, ut pauxillum ad refocillandam animam cibi caperent'.
[39] *Ibid.*, I.21,2 and I.25,1.
[40] This, incidentally, is one of the passages which show that Gildas is speaking of a limited area of Britain: it is inconceivable that the entire island was fighting itself for food. Gildas is referring to the damage done by the Picts and Irish before 446, and in my view he has northern Britain in mind.

when Eugippius's narrative opens.[41] We might have thought, then, that here as in Britain civil wars would have been fought as the provincials struggled to lay hands on their neighbours' food-supplies or as individuals struggled for power and position. Perhaps not unconnected with the civil wars are the 'tyrants' who sprang up in such quantities in the parts of Britain not yet occupied by the Saxons and who are exceedingly rare elsewhere. Gildas first mentions these 'kings', as he sometimes calls them, as arising several years after 446.[42] But we hear of no such civil wars or of any such 'tyrants' in Noricum Ripense even though Eugippius's detailed and illuminating narrative covers most of the second half of the fifth century. There were two 'tyrants' in north-east Spain, one at the very end of the fifth century, the other at the beginning of the sixth.[43] We know hardly anything about them except that they did not survive for long and that they are not reported to have engaged in wars against other Hispano-Romans. Presumably, they hoped to organise some resistance to the Visigoths. In Gaul a pocket of free, unconquered territory was left behind by the advancing barbarians, and its ruler from 465 to 486/7, Syagrius, was known as 'king of the Romans', *rex Romanorum*; but since his function was not to fight other Gallo-Romans but to protect his territory against the barbarians, he is very different from the 'kings' of whom Gildas speaks.[44] On the other hand, as the Saxons encroached farther and farther into Britain civil wars among the Britons became endemic. This must have added to conditions in the island a degree of horror and gruesome ferocity which the other Western provinces were spared. And these civil wars continued unabated even after the victory – a purely local victory, as far as we can judge – over the barbarians, or one group of them, which had been won at Mount Badon.[45] But if you agree that the explanation of the events of 409 is that put forward above,[46] that the struggle was an open class-war, then we could account for the ferocity of the civil wars of which Gildas speaks, a ferocity which was unequalled on the Continent and which did not abate even in the teeth of the Saxon advance. Wars of this intensity, fought by the victors of 409 among themselves or fought by the victors against dispossessed landowners trying to regain their estates, might well destroy city-life even in districts where the word 'Saxon' still meant a barbarian living on the other side of the Rhine.

Be that as it may, the 'strong men' established themselves in Britain to such an extent that Procopius, writing in Byzantium in the middle of the sixth century, believed that after 410 Britain was ruled exclusively by usurpers, 'tyrants', although he is far from clear about the great invasions which had overwhelmed the former Roman diocese by the time when he was

[41] Thompson, *Romans and Barbarians*, p. 118f.
[42] Gildas, *De Excidio*, I.21,4.
[43] *Chronicle of Saragossa*, *s.aa.* 496, 506 (ed. Mommsen, *Chronica Minora*, II.222).
[44] On Syagrius see Jones *et al.*, *The Prosopography*, II.1041f.
[45] Gildas, *De Excidio*, I.26,2.
[46] See pp. 32–4 above.

writing.[47] The successors of the fifth-century tyrants still held sway in the unoccupied parts of Britain at the time when he and Gildas were writing, and a thoroughly brutal lot they appear to have been. We have no means of knowing when exactly these men established their power (apart from Gildas's remark that they were in existence not long after the appeal to Aetius in 446);[48] but Procopius seems to have thought that they followed on more or less directly after the events of 409/10, and as regards some parts of Britain his view may well be right. In Gildas's day there were at least five of them along the western seaboard between Devon and Anglesey. They often fought and conquered one another; but we never hear that a number of them combined to defeat the Saxon invaders, although this may be due to the fact that those of whom Gildas had information lived far away from those battlefields and the barbarian settlements; and Gildas was probably ignorant of what was happening farther east. On the other hand, we never hear that any of them called upon the Saxons (or the Irish) to help him against his rivals and opponents, although once again they may have been saved by geography rather than by any high moral principles. Had they lived closer to the invaders, their dealings with them (at any rate, in the sixth century) might have been less reputable. In the first fifty years and more of the fifth century it is hard to believe that any Briton would have called upon the Picts or Saxons for help: the one example of which we do know – the proud tyrant of the North – may have set a clear warning to the others.

In addition to the famines and the civil wars and the odious tyrants there was another surprising difference between the course of events in Britain and that which the other Western provinces experienced. This concerns the fate of the cities. We are tolerably well supplied with descriptions of some other Western provinces as they were in process of being overrun by the barbarians in the fifth century – such provinces as Gaul, Spain, and Noricum.

During the forty years between 429, when the Vandals left Spain for Africa, and 469, when Hydatius's chronicle comes to an end, the Sueves in Galicia were the only barbarians in Spain. They ranked as weak and few in comparison with the Vandals, who themselves ranked as weak in comparison with the other major Germanic peoples.[49] Now, it was an event of extreme rarity for the Sueves to capture a Hispano-Roman city. In fact, in these forty years only half-a-dozen cities fell to them (although two of them fell more than once). And yet the Sueves were sending out marauding parties prac- tically every year, at any rate after 438. When a powerful force of Visigoths, led by their king himself, invaded Spain in 455/6 they brought the total of captured cities up from six to ten, but the Visigoths at this date could put into the field a far more developed and efficient army – on this campaign it included many Romans – than anything that the Saxons could even dream of. The essential point to notice is that not one of these fallen Spanish cities is

[47] Procopius, *Bellum Vandalicum*, III.2,38, with Thompson, 'Procopius', p. 506.
[48] Gildas, *De Excidio*, I.21,4.
[49] Salvian, *De Gubernatione Dei*, VII.27f.

known to have been defended. In several cases, to be sure, we do not know *how* the cities came to fall. For example, one Suevic king took two provincial capitals, Merida and Seville, in 439 and 441 respectively, and we do not know how he managed to do so. Hydatius, far away in the north-west of the Iberian peninsula, may not have been able to find out how it was done; but if there had been a siege and a sack he might well have heard of it and would probably have told us. Certainly, the terms which he uses would hardly suggest that the two cities were stormed.[50] In fact, the capture of a defended Roman city was recognised to be so difficult that the Sueves are never reported even to have tried to take one. A place called Martylum was indeed besieged by one of the Suevic kings. It must have been a very small settlement indeed, for it cannot now be identified – and it is not even clear that the king was able to take it.[51] When the Visigoths attacked an otherwise unknown fort called *Couiacense castrum*, thirty Roman miles from Astorga, they were worn down by the long struggle which ensued and retreated with heavy losses.[52] Similarly, civilians in Noricum often occupied the old military forts (*castella*) for refuge, and these the barbarians were never able to take in the thirty years covered by Eugippius's *Life*.[53]

How then did the barbarians in Spain manage to take the cities which did fall to them? Hydatius reports two methods. Some they took by a trick, *sub specie pacis, per dolum, dolose, in pace decepta*.[54] As for the Visigoths, we know how they took Astorga. A number of 'brigands', *praedones* – presumably Hispano-Roman brigands, for Hydatius does not refer to the Sueves as simply *praedones* or *latrones* or the like[55] – gave out that they had been ordered by the Roman authorities to enter the place, and so gained admission.[56] That was also how the Visigoths were able to enter the town: they said that the Roman authorities had instructed them to fight the remaining Sueves, and the simple-hearted Astorgans swallowed this bait and opened the gates to them. Presumably this is the trick, the *dolus*, which led to the fall of the other cities, too, to the Sueves. That is how they took the cities *sub specie pacis*. Perhaps that was how the Vandals captured Carthage itself on 19 October 439.[57]

The second way in which the barbarians took some Spanish cities was treachery on the part of one or more of the inhabitants.[58] But that happened only at a relatively late stage of the invasions. In the later fifth century some Spaniards and Gauls – men like Seronatus and Arvandus in Gaul and Lusidius of Lisbon – began to see that the future lay with the barbarian rulers of their country and that the days of Roman power were a thing of the

---

[50] Hydatius, *Chronicle*, § 119, *ingreditur* (Merida); § 123, *obtenta* (Seville).
[51] *Ibid.*, § 121.
[52] *Ibid.*, § 186.
[53] Thompson, *Romans and Barbarians*, p. 122.
[54] Hydatius, *Chronicle*, §§ 188, 201, 142, 229, 241.
[55] But what is the meaning of *praedones ipsius* in Hydatius, *Chronicle*, § 186?
[56] *Ibid.*, § 186, 'sub specie Romanae ordinationis'.
[57] Prosper, *Chronicon*, § 1339 (ed. Mommsen, *Chronica Minora*, I.477), *dolo pacis*; Hydatius, *Chronicle*, § 115 (*ibid.*, I.23).
[58] Hydatius, *Chronicle*, §§ 201, 246.

past: hence the best course was to face facts, to enter the new rulers' service, and to make the best of a bad job. And so, later on in 469, the year in which he betrayed Lisbon to the Sueves, we find Lusidius serving as one of the Suevic king's envoys to the emperor and travelling far away to Italy.[59] Indeed, it was even said that Rome itself fell to the Visigoths on 24 August 410 because it had been betrayed.[60]

A third way in which the cities fell to the barbarians is mentioned in Eugippius's *Life* of St Severinus. In Noricum some cities were taken by surprise (although the Spaniards had evidently taken precautions against this, as we do not hear of cities being surprised there). Batavis (Passau) was surprised by a handful of barbarians at a time when the population at large was busy with the harvest and only forty men had been left to guard the town.[61] Two tiny places of minimal importance called Asturis and Ioviaco were surprised.[62] Quintanis was taken by surprise, but only when the majority of the inhabitants had migrated to another town.[63] A considerable number of Norican towns did *not* fall to the attackers – for example, Comagenis, Favianis, Tiburnia (the provincial capital of Noricum Mediterraneum), Lauriacum, and (before most of its inhabitants had left it) Quintanis. Yet all of these places had been attacked. The case of Quintanis is instructive, for it illustrates a fourth manner in which the barbarians could destroy the life of a Roman city. It was not stormed, but the raids of the Alamanni had been so frequent that the inhabitants were worn out and eventually were forced to abandon the town and migrate elsewhere. If the crops could not be sown or reaped and if the cattle had been driven away or their fodder exhausted, there was nothing left for the townsmen to do but to emigrate to some less harassed city, as the Noricans often did, or else, like the Britons (according to Gildas), they could take to the mountains, the woods, and the caves.[64] There is no direct evidence – nor could there be – that any British town fell for this reason, but it is by no means impossible that many may in fact have done so. The process would mean that the abandoned town would show to archaeologists no trace of violent assault or of storm, and indeed no British town has revealed any such traces. This form of destruction does not necessarily imply the presence of barbarians: internal enemies could well bring about the same result.

The barbarians, then, took the Continental Roman cities in general (i) by pretending that the Roman authorities had sent them to take part in the defence, (ii) by treachery on the part of some of the citizens, (iii) by rushing them and taking them by surprise, and (iv) by overrunning the adjacent

---

[59] *Ibid.*, § 351.
[60] Sozomen, *Historia Ecclesiastica*, IX.9,4; cf. Procopius, *Bellum Vandalicum*, I.2,27. Contrast Jerome, *Epistulae*, 127,12.
[61] Eugippius, *Vita S. Seuerini*, § 22,4.
[62] *Ibid.*, I.2, *insidiae*; 24,3.
[63] *Ibid.*, 28,3.
[64] Gildas, *De Excidio*, I.20,2; Eugippius, *Vita S. Seuerini*, § 27, 1. Cf. the sufferings of the citizens of Clermont Ferrand as reported by Sidonius: see Stevens, *Sidonius*, pp. 141–60.

countryside and destroying the crops so systematically and so frequently year after year that the citizens (who would have starved if they had stayed) were obliged to migrate even though their town walls were intact. But, of course, (v) there was also a fifth way of entering the cities: sometimes the barbarians stormed them, and to that method we shall return in a moment. But few British cities will have fallen in the early years of the invasions for three of the other four reasons which I have listed. True, it may well be that some British cities fell to the Saxons because of repeated and systematic destruction of the food-supply and the livestock and the fodder at a time when stores could not be imported from elsewhere. Such catastrophes would be one way of accounting for the absence of burnt debris from the archaeological finds. But I doubt whether any British city fell in the early years of the invasions for the other three reasons given by our Continental authorities. In the first years of the Saxon landings the Britons would know that no ruler, however crass, would employ Saxons newly out of their boats to attack other Saxons or to garrison the walls of a British town. (The proud tyrant may to some extent be an exception to this generalisation, for he did indeed import Saxon 'defenders', although it is in the last degree unlikely that he planted them in the northern towns, since they knew nothing of siege-warfare – and their function was to repel Picts, not Saxons.) In general, however, the citizens would hardly admit within their walls any band of Saxons who claimed to have been sent by the local ruler to defend them. The wonder is rather that the simple-hearted Spaniards were so often hoodwinked in this way. Nor is it easy to see how any Briton in the first half of the fifth century, whether slave or free, would have had an interest in betraying his city to these brutal raiders.[65] The Britons were soon to learn by experience that if they did surrender to the Saxons – if, for example, hunger forced them to surrender – they were as likely as not to be cut down in cold blood.[66] But in the days of St Germanus, and long after them, few Britons can have realised that the future lay with the Saxons, and fewer still will either have wished to join them or even have thought of so doing.

But, of course, many cities of the Continental provinces were taken by storm. Trier itself, for long the military capital of north-west Europe, the richest city of Gaul, was stormed (*expugnata*) four times by the barbarians.[67] Zosimus tells us that in the chaotic conditions following on the overthrow of the usurper Magnentius in 353 the Franks, Alamanni, and Saxons captured 'forty' Gallic cities standing on the Rhine. But apparently they did not storm

---

[65] I do not know why Johnson, *Later Roman Britain*, p. 105, writes thus of the British revolt of 409: 'If Britain's rebellion was really a Bacaudic one, then the Bacaudae ought to have joined with the Saxons to overthrow the cities'. Collaboration between Bacaudae and barbarian invaders in the field is exceedingly rarely reported in our sources, the only explicit case being that reported from Spain in 449: see Hydatius, *Chronicle*, § 142 (ed. Mommsen, *Chronica Minora*, II.25). It would be more than a little rash to generalise from that one incident. For collaboration between Romans (especially traders) and invaders see Thompson, 'Barbarian invaders'.

[66] Gildas, *De Excidio*, I.25,1.

[67] Salvian, *De Gubernatione Dei*, VI.39 & 74 (cf. 82).

them. The Caesar Julian writes that 'every' city and fort on the Rhine was abandoned by its garrison and so was handed over undefended to the Franks and Saxons, 'the most warlike of the nations around the Rhine and the Western Sea'.[68] When provincial cities did fall, they may have done so for all sorts of reasons, some of them unexpected. For example, when the Persian king attacked the city of Amida in Mesopotamia in 502, the defence of one of the city-towers was in the hands of a group of monks, and at the moment when the attack was launched – and it was directed particularly at their tower – these monks were so drunk that they were unaware even that an attack was in progress.[69] I suspect that the sober-sided Britons rarely entrusted the defence of their cities to parties of intoxicated monks! But the Britons too, no doubt, will have had their share of surprises.

The evidence from the Continent does not prepare us for what Gildas tells us. He mentions neither tricks nor treachery. According to him, the barbarians took the cities by storm.[70] They do not seem to have hesitated to attack the walled cities even when these were defended; and this applies to the Picts as well as to the Saxons. The barbarians from beyond Hadrian's Wall dragged the citizens off the city-walls by means of 'barbed missiles' (uncinata tela,[71] a nice problem, these: for no Western people is known to have used barbed spears in this way at this date, although barbed spearheads had been well known among the Germanic peoples for centuries and were used by Germanic troops serving in the Roman army in Britain even in the third and fourth centuries).[72] The cities were abandoned, the citizens scattered, there were cruel massacres.[73] That is to say, the Picts achieved once or perhaps often what was a comparative rarity for the Germans on the Continent – the storming of a walled and defended city (although its defenders were not professional soldiers, but civilians).

The Saxon Federates of the proud tyrant, when they rebelled, likewise devasted 'town and country'.[74] Agrosque in this passage is Gildas's only reference to the fate of the countryside. On the villas he is silent, and it is well known that 'he knew nothing whatever of villas. They had passed from the scene so long before his time that not even a tradition was left.'[75] It is ominous that in eastern Britain not a single Roman estate-name survived

[68] Zosimus, *History*, III.1; Julian, *Oration* I.35A.
[69] Procopius, *Bellum Persicum*, I.7,23.
[70] I do not understand *in edito arcis* in *De Excidio*, I.19,2. Is he referring in these sentences to one specific walled town or to several? With the words 'quid plura?' he certainly moves on to discuss the general experience. Ammianus does not quite say that the Picts captured the British cities in 367/8: *History*, XXVIII.3,2, 'in integrum restituit [*sc.* Theodosius] ciuitates et castra, multiplicibus quidem damnis afflicta'; 7, 'instaurabat urbes et praesidiaria (ut diximus) castra'. The most which we can legitimately deduce from these remarks is that the barbarians had managed to damage some of the cities and that Theodosius now repaired this damage in addition to undoing the results of prolonged neglect during the previous generations.
[71] Gildas, *De Excidio*, I.19,2.
[72] Swanton, *The Spearheads*, pp. 21f. and 139.
[73] Gildas, *De Excidio*, I.19,3.
[74] *Ibid.*, I.24,1.
[75] Frere, *Britannia*, p. 419.

into later times.[76] Nor did any Roman village-name. But as for the cities, Gildas says that all of these (*cunctae coloniae*) were taken by means of battering-rams,[77] and all the citizens were massacred, the priests as well as the people. Gildas mentions this last point because he seems to hold the remarkable view that it is a more heinous crime to murder a priest than to murder a farmer or a shopkeeper.[78] He calls the city-dwellers *coloni*, a term that would have been less than flattering if he had known what it meant – and it is interesting that he did not know what it meant.

The tradition which reached Gildas, then, told of the widespread sack of cities, but not until *ca* 440 and later; and it is not easy to see how such a tradition could possibly have reached him, writing less than a hundred years after the events, unless it is essentially true. The British towns, in fact, in the area of which he had information were in general not taken either by guile or by surprise or by treachery or by repeated loss of their crops, like the Spanish and Norican towns: they were stormed. The cities on the Rhine fell because they were not defended. The British cities fell although they *were* defended, admittedly by civilians, men who were not supported by the organisation, training, and equipment of the Imperial army.

Nothing in all this contradicts the view of those archaeologists who assure us that city-life continued in several places into the middle of the fifth century. It is true that there is, and can be, no agreement on what constitutes 'city-life' in this context. Were the markets still held there regularly? Were the markets permanent? Were considerable bodies of merchants and professional, full-time craftsmen still active? Were the towns in any sense centres of administration? Did the town-council (*curia*) still meet? Did it arrange for the collection of taxes and the administration of justice? None of these or similar questions about the years after 410 can be answered with any assurance in the case of any British city. Indeed, it is not out of the question that in some cases the cities may only have been places of refuge in a moment of crisis. In other places people may have lived in them as small groups of independent families, or as refugees waiting for times to get better, or even as detached individuals, squatters, no longer forming an organised hierarchical community. But if there was only a handful of scattered inhabitants on any one site, then it is easy to see how the Picts and Saxons alike might have been able to storm the towns. The British towns may have fallen because there were fewer people in them than in the towns of Spain (before 469, when our information dries up) or of Noricum (before 483, when Eugippius's evidence ends). The defenders were very few indeed, so few that they could not even destroy from their walls the Saxon assailants who were rushing battering-rams against their gates. And with the disappearance of professional soldiers,

[76] Jackson, *Language and History*, p. 233.
[77] Gildas, *De Excidio*, I.24,3f., where Winterbottom (*Gildas*, p. 27) translates *coloniae* as 'major towns'; but I doubt whether Gildas knew what a *colonia* was or had been in earlier days. The status of *colonia* meant little or nothing after Diocletian: see Jones, *The Greek City*, p. 147.
[78] *De Excidio*, I.24,3.

no doubt the use of the great catapults, the *ballistae*, which could have defended the cities, had also disappeared. We do not know how many British cities were involved in the raids of which Gildas is speaking; but even allowing for the exaggerations of a rhetorician, the number cannot have been negligible. He even says *cunctae coloniae*,[79] as though to be stormed by the barbarians were the normal or even universal experience of the British cities. True, Gildas can never speak, as far as we can see, about the experience of Britain as a whole from the Channel to Hadrian's Wall or from the Wash to the Irish Sea. He knows only the history of the region neighbouring upon the place where he was writing. But in and around that 'region', as he calls it more than once, there is no reason to doubt that the invaders were able to storm several towns; and if they did so there, why not throughout the whole of eastern Britain? But Gildas is referring to the years after *ca* 440. He gives no reason for thinking that the storming of British cities began directly after 410.

The Arian Visigoths sacked Braga on Sunday, 28 October 455. They took many Hispano-Roman prisoners, wrecked the (Catholic) churches, broke the altars, carried off nuns but did not violate them, stripped clergymen naked, dragged men, women, and children out of their places of refuge, filled the holy places with horses, cattle, and – rather unexpectedly – camels.[80] What is truly astonishing is that Hydatius, who tells us all this, adds that on this occasion there was no bloodshed, *incruenta . . . direptio*. (It was very different when they took Astorga during that same campaign.) Again, when the Sueves took Conimbrica by treachery in 468 they demolished houses and part of the city-wall, but Hydatius makes no reference to bloodshed: the inhabitants were taken prisoner or they left the place and scattered, and for the time being the town was left desolate.[81] Indeed, there is a remarkable number of entries in Hydatius's chronicle where we might have expected a reference to bloodshed but find none.[82] It may well be that in the numerous cases where Hydatius makes no reference to bloodshed, few lives were in fact lost, although it would be optimistic to suppose that these raids were literally bloodless. On the other hand, it would be wholly incorrect to say that the barbarians wiped out urban life in Spain in the middle of the fifth century, even though they left Conimbrica momentarily desolate.

Gildas says that the invaders burned the cities. He gives a vivid description of those cities which were taken by the Saxons and of their condition in his day: they had been 'deserted and demolished',[83] but not by any means wholly demolished: they remained an impressive sight with their great walls, towers, and gateways,[84] even though these had been damaged. The amount

[79] *Ibid.*
[80] Hydatius, *Chronicle*, § 174 (ed. Mommsen, *Chronica Minora*, II. 29).
[81] *Ibid.*, § 241.
[82] *Ibid.*, § § 119, 142, 168, 170, 193, 202, 219, 229, 246, 249f. Contrast § § 188 (the slaughter of Romans by Sueves in Lusitania in 457), 198, 199.
[83] *De Excidio*, I.26,2, *desertae dirutaeque*; cf. I.2, *de urbium subuersione*.
[84] *Ibid.*, I.3,2.

of damage which could be done to stone-built houses and enormous public buildings and monumental defensive walls, even with the help of fire, was limited, especially as the attackers at any one time on any one site were probably few in number and in the early days starving, as likely as not. After plundering the contents of the towns the marauders had no interest in lingering idly in order gratuitously to damage, still less demolish, the empty and looted buildings. They might light a few random fires – and the thatched roofs of the private houses would blaze as readily for them as they had done by accident when Germanus was in one of them – but very soon they would have to go on their way to search for some other supply of food and loot.[85]

When they had gone, no doubt dead bodies and purple blood, as Gildas assures us,[86] could be seen in the streets. Accordingly, when archaeologists find evidence that the forum and basilica of Silchester, the basilica at Caerwent, and the centre of Wroxeter ended in a fire, while a house in Caistor-by-Norwich appears to have endured a fire and to have been the scene of a massacre, and again when they find the remains of unburied bodies lying in the streets of Caerwent, Cirencester, and Wroxeter, it is not easy to see why they are reluctant to cite Gildas to interpret their ghoulish finds or why they gravely assure us that the bodies left lying unburied in a street in Cirencester died of a plague![87] The picture is precisely that which Gildas draws, although it by no means follows that he had these particular cities in mind.

Of one phenomenon Gildas reveals no knowledge whatever. It never seems to occur to him that the Saxons might have planned to settle *inside* the abandoned British cities or that some of them were already living in the cities before the catastrophe broke over them. On the contrary, he is quite clear that the cities, although their fortifications and buildings were impressive in his own day, were then empty and uninhabited whether by Roman survivors or by Saxon newcomers. Only the wild beasts and the birds of prey lived in them.[88] To be sure, he can speak for only one 'region' of Britain, apparently the north; but wherever we may think that he lived, he is not likely to have been in touch with the cities of the South-east, which suffered the first and most furious onslaught of the invaders. If he speaks, then, of the destruction of the cities in his region of Britain we may be sure that the cities farther to the east and south had met an even more terrible fate.[89]

In fact, the relationship of the invaders in the early days with the British

---

[85] But notice *incendiis* in Ammianus Marcellinus, *History*, XXVII.8,5, where the word may include the burning of crops, farm-buildings, and so on as well as of cities, although no cities are there said to have been taken. Salvian, *De Gubernatione Dei*, VI.82, says of Trier *cumque omnis ciuitas combusta esset*.

[86] *De Excidio*, I.24,3.

[87] Wacher, *The Towns*, p. 389. See further Salvian, *De Gubernatione Dei*, VI.84, who had seen – and smelt – the dead bodies in the streets of Trier.

[88] *De Excidio*, I.3,2 and I.24,3.

[89] The occurrence of a city-name in an early text by no means proves continuity: Alcock, *Arthur's Britain*, p. 186f.

cities has been the subject of misunderstanding. Archaeologists often use language which suggests that the Saxons could have taken over the cities for their own occupation if they had wished to do so but that they voluntarily decided not to live in them. The famous sentiment reported by Ammianus Marcellinus[90] that the Alamanni (a Germanic people living east of the Rhine and south of the Main) avoided 'the cities themselves as being tombs surrounded by nets' ought not to suggest that the Alamanni could have occupied and inhabited the seven cities of which the historian is speaking here – if only they had had a mind to do so, if only they had had a different subjective attitude to cities, or if they had not been held back by superstition, or if they had not feared military surprise when once they had settled in them. It was not a matter of subjective choice. The Alamanni had indeed started to live on the land in the *territoria* of these seven cities, but as for the cities themselves they had no choice in the matter. If the techniques of production and the division of labour among the Alamanni or the Saxons had been developed far enough to require and demand urban life, there would no doubt have been Alamannic and Saxon cities in their homelands before they ever moved into the Roman provinces; and in fact there were none. The Saxons could indeed have inhabited the British cities if they had been capable of producing regularly a surplus of commodities which they were obliged to exchange for the surplus of other commodities produced by other communities. Did they need permanent markets? They would also have had to be able to support full-time specialist artisans and craftsmen whose techniques had been sufficiently advanced for them to produce more of their own goods than their household or clan or even their village required: they would then be obliged to take their surplus to market. (It is not easy to state the preconditions of urban life in a couple of sentences!) It is more than unlikely that the Saxons of the early fifth century could have met these and similar conditions. Even full-time professional potters could hardly be found among them at this date. Early Saxon pottery was not thrown on the wheel; and in primitive societies the use of hand-made pottery tends to mean that it was made by women for use in the household, not by specialised male potters for sale on the market. There can hardly be said to be a 'market' for pottery at this date. Whether some of these female potters may or may not have been British captives, no one knows. It seems to be the case that in the decade 410–20 the most active British potteries went out of production, and some households – or their womenfolk – produced their own pottery. But whether the pots were made by women or by men, by Britons or by Saxons, who can tell? And who is to say which pot made in these conditions is 'British' and which is 'Saxon'?[91] Certainly, Saxon smiths, too, can hardly have been very numerous in the early days: weapons and implements and even pots would

[90] Ammianus Marcellinus, *History*, XVI.2,12. But notice Salvian, *De Gubernatione Dei*, VI.39, on Köln as being *hostibus plena*: for how long?

[91] Note Frere's conclusion (*Britannia*, p. 419) that 'the pottery, often handmade, shows . . . that native potters were working for new masters'. See p. 97, n. 27, above.

have been taken as loot whenever possible,[92] and a captive British smith would be a very prized possession indeed. In the earliest and hungriest days of the invasions the mining of metals by the invaders would have been out of the question. And as for the towns as administrative centres, it would be a very long time indeed before such were required by the starving and illiterate invaders. Nor was there any inducement to live in stone houses needing repairs which the Saxons could not carry out. And, although many of the early marauding bands may have taken shelter in an intact Roman barn, what Saxon farmer would voluntarily live in the middle of some acres of collapsed or tottering masonry? The first invaders will certainly have made straight for the British settlements, villages, farms in their desperate need for food,[93] and according to Gildas they managed to storm some of the cities; but it is clear that any period of joint occupation of the cities by Britons and Saxons was (if we may judge from the evidence of our literary authorities) an impossibility. The question of the 'continuity' of the Romano-British cities in the eastern part of the country is a false problem. There never was, and never could have been, a time in the fifth century when the persons walking this way and that along the streets of a Romano-British town were speaking, some of them a Germanic language, and the others a Celtic language or Latin. The question why the Saxons did not adopt urban life as soon as they disembarked from their boats is not a problem at all. On the other hand, a very real problem – and one which I have never seen discussed – is why urban life now became impossible for the Britons and why the cities were still lying desolate in Gildas's day even as far west as the region where he was writing. I am thinking of those areas of Britain which the Saxon invaders had not yet reached at the time when he took up his pen. Even there, it seems, urban life had become impossible. Why? According to Gildas, it was the Saxon attacks which ended the life of the British cities, but this destruction by the invaders was not definitive: what prevented the revival of the cities was the civil wars which the Britons continued to fight.[94] Was that true also of the western cities which were still untouched by the Saxons?

A radical difference between the settlement of the barbarians in Britain and the various settlements in Gaul was that the Visigoths and Burgundians were planted on the Gallo-Roman estates in a controlled and indeed agreed manner and under carefully formulated rules which did not entail the complete expropriation of the Gallo-Roman landed gentry. The barbarians, or at any rate their leaders, were given a stake in the land and in the exploitation of those who worked it. The management of the landed estates, like the civil administration of the provinces in which the barbarians were settled, and also the municipal organisation, remained in essentials as the emperors had left them; and they continued to be controlled by Romans. The ownership of

---

[92] There are some judicious remarks on iron-production in the earliest days of the settlements in Swanton, *The Spearheads*, p. 140f.

[93] See p. 96f. above.

[94] Gildas, *De Excidio*, I.26,2.

some parts of the larger estates was transferred to new, barbarian landlords, and the supply of agricultural labour was replenished by the newcomers. In due course changes were made, at the highest level of the old provincial administration, so as to bring the system under the control of the kings. But the major change brought about by the settlement of the Continental Federates concerned the armed forces: these were commanded by the barbarian leaders and their function was to protect the province in which they had been settled – that is, to protect Roman and barbarian inhabitants alike against all threats from outside. In due course, public matters were conducted by the king and the chief landowners, Roman as well as barbarian. The kings quickly published codes of law, and these laws they enforced by means of their armed strength.

The barbarians lived under their own leaders and laws and in theory had no control over their Roman neighbours. Now, these barbarians were far more highly developed socially than the Saxons and were far more familiar with Roman ideas of law and government. The Visigoths, for example, had been living in the Roman provinces for over forty years before the Patrician Constantius planted them as Federates in Aquitaine. They could take over Roman society as a going concern and keep it going. Their leaders had accommodated themselves to Roman society and were in process of seizing for themselves a higher degree of political power over their barbarian followers and more social prestige in their own societies than anything which they had known in earlier days or which the Saxon tribal nobility would know for decades to come.[95] The literary sources give us a very different picture of Saxon society (in so far as they give us a picture at all). According to them, the fifth-century Saxons lived in a society composed of a large number of groups (whether kinship-groups, retinues, or other conglomerations) among which any sort of chieftainship was difficult for an outsider to detect, an illiterate society without political development, which could not hold masses of slaves, still less govern and exploit a subject population.

Accordingly, on the Continent, Roman life under barbarian rule was possible and tolerable and in some cases (though hardly for Catholics in Vandal Africa) even preferable to life under the corrupt tax-collectors of the Imperial government. To be sure, since the Roman administration continued to function under the barbarian kings, the Roman taxes continued to be collected just as Roman law continued to be administered among the Roman subjects of the kings. But the illiterate Saxons could not even begin to govern the British population. They could certainly not collect the taxes or administer the law; and few will think that the Roman machinery for collecting taxes survived the middle of the century. They could not even extract a regular tribute from any Britons whom they might have subjected. They had no organisation for the collection of tribute and, according to Procopius, the collection of tribute was rare even in the sixth century among

[95] Thompson, *Romans and Barbarians*, pp. 38–57.

the Germanic barbarians on the Danubian frontier of the Empire.[96] They were equally unable to administer a Roman landed estate. So when we read in the modern literature such a sentence as 'the bulk of the British peasantry must have stayed where it was and passed under the political or tenurial control of the Saxon lords and their followers', we may wonder how a larger number of questions could possibly be begged in so few words![97]

In northwestern Spain, however, the Sueves had settled without being planted there as Federates. In the middle of the fifth century there were two capital differences between these Sueves who ravaged Spain and the Saxons who had landed in Britain. The Sueves appear to have been remarkably few. The guess that there were as many as 20,000 or 25,000 of them, men, women, and children, may well be an overstatement.[98] We do not know the number of the invading Saxons at any one time during the fifth century but, as the decades went by, many tens of thousands of them must have landed in Britain, even though no doubt they normally came in dribs and drabs – three boatloads here and five boatloads there, and so on, but in far larger fleets from time to time when conditions were ripe, as perhaps in 446/7. Thus the pressure on the Britons was relentless, and it never ended. If the Britons disposed of one band of raiders, it was only a matter of time, probably of a short time, before they were faced with two or three more. Secondly, the Sueves raided Spain looking for loot. They were mere plunderers. They did not try to extend their dominions in the period which Hydatius's chronicle covers. The Saxons, too, were looking for loot and for food but, from the mid-forties, as we have guessed, they also wanted land on a large scale to settle on; and that is the crucial difference between the Sueves and the Saxons. Every winter the Sueves went back to their homes in Gallaecia. There came a time, however, when the bulk of the Saxon raiders did not return to the Continent but overwintered in Britain, as no doubt smaller groups had done before. The aim now was conquest and settlement. If we had a British chronicle like that of Hydatius, covering the central years of the fifth century in Britain, we may guess that the word *incruenta*[99] would not have been used in it very often. But in northwestern Spain the Sueves altered nothing. The Latin language, the place-names, the christian religion have survived there from that day to this. What we need and do not possess is an account of some region of Europe where the language and religion were wiped out by the Germanic invaders as thoroughly as they were obliterated by the Saxons in eastern England. We should like to have a description of what happened, for example, in the German-speaking lands (as they now are but were not in Roman times) on the left bank of the Rhine or in northern

[96] See Thompson, *The Early Germans*, p. 69f.: Procopius, *Bellum Gothicum*, VI.14,9.

[97] The quotation is from the otherwise interesting paper of Taylor, 'The Anglo-Saxon countryside', p. 6.

[98] Thompson, *Romans and Barbarians*, p. 158. There are some remarks *ibid.*, pp. 212–17, on the differences between the fates of Roman Spain and Roman Britain.

[99] See p. 107 above.

Switzerland. How did the course of events there compare or contrast with what happened in eastern England?

At all events, the position in eastern England was very different indeed from that in Spanish Gallaecia. To my mind, it is incredible that the bulk of the British peasants stayed where they were, as even the Galicians did. It is true that many pockets of Britons were left behind by the advancing Saxons: place-names have revealed the existence of scores of such British communities.[100] Many students assert that these formed something like the bulk of the population as a whole. But if the Saxon invasion of eastern England were a matter of peaceful co-existence over a period of years, as is increasingly thought, how could we explain the disappearance of the place-names (other than those of prominent natural or manmade features – Roman cities, large rivers, hills, forests)? How could we account for the utter disappearance of the Celtic language from eastern England and of the christian religion?[101] How could we account for the fact that only about a score of nouns made their way from British Celtic into Anglo-Saxon and none at all from British Latin? Why did the Saxons fail to borrow as simple a device as the potter's wheel? Why did tens of thousands of Britons flee to the Continent as early as the 460s? Why was it that the Britons who survived in the west of the island conceived a hatred of the Saxons which the passage of generations and even of centuries did little to abate? Why, in fact, did they refuse to preach the Gospel to their tormentors even in the early eighth century, a fact which shocked Bede?[102] In view of all this and much besides, I do not know how it can be inferred that 'in point of fact the British population was nowhere completely exterminated'.[103] On the contrary, the pockets of survivors must have been the exceptions; and Jackson allows that the fact that *walh*-names were given at all to British surviving communities implies that they were the exception, very much the exception.[104]

It has also been held that the Britons in general in the eastern region learned English, and learned it so thoroughly and so accurately that they 'mangled', as Jackson puts it, British names so as to suit the sound-system of the invaders.[105] But what were the social conditions which brought about this improbable state of affairs? Why should vast numbers of British survivors (if vast numbers of them existed) have learned to speak flawless, perfect English in addition to their own Celtic? The vast majority of Britons had certainly not learned Latin, even a little Latin (to say nothing of perfect, flawless Latin), during the four hundred years of Imperial rule. Why should they now

[100] Cameron, 'The meaning'. In each of the cases which he discusses we know the Saxon place-name only, the British name having wholly and universally disappeared. In other words, each of these communities without exception was either absorbed or eliminated by the invaders.
[101] On a handful of exceptions to this last matter see Cameron, 'Eccles', and cf. Jackson, *Language and History*, p. 227; Thomas, *Christianity*, pp. 262–6.
[102] *Historia Ecclesiastica*, II.20.
[103] Jackson, *Language and History*, p. 234.
[104] *Ibid.*, p. 235.
[105] *Ibid.*, p. 242; cf. p. 245.

– overnight, we might say – attend advanced classes on primitive Old English? All the data can be adequately explained if we suppose that in many Saxon communities of the South and East there was a relatively small number of British slaves and servants, most of them women and children in the first generation of the invasions, a few of them adult males whose kinsmen and neighbours had disappeared or had been wiped out and who were themselves of some service to the invaders. Now, at the other side of the Roman Empire, the Austurian nomads, who used to raid Cyrenaica, would prize no possession more highly than a Roman woman captive and her child: the women prisoners would bear them sons who would one day strengthen their levies, while the male children, when they grew up, would also fight for them 'for they become loyal to those who brought them up instead of to their parents'. So the children who were now carried off captive would one day come back to ravage the land which bore them.[106] Is it surprising that some 'Saxon' warriors, and later on 'Saxon' leaders, bore Celtic names? The evidence does not support the view that the invaders made a clean sweep of the Britons in the east of the island, but it does suggest that from the British point of view the position was not much better. It is easy enough to understand, then, why Constantius found it so hard to discover the truth about what had happened to Germanus during his visits to the island and also why information about Britain in his own day scarcely existed in his part of Gaul.

Fortunately, it has been given to few writers to draw as dark a picture as that which Gildas sketches of the Britain of his day – or of that limited part of Britain about which he had information. Less than a century ago a colossal civilisation collapsed into the dust. Its great cities with their stone buildings and massive fortifications and crenellated towers[107] are still in the main standing. Although some towers have been thrown down, the cities are still impressive; but there is no living creature inside them except the wild beasts and the birds which have made their lairs there. The descendants of the survivors of the catastrophe no longer live in cities: for them, whatever the reason may have been, life in cities is no longer possible. Even in the west of the island life has reverted to a pre-urban stage. The merchant, the retailer, the administrator, the rich man with his servants visiting his town house, the tax-collector, judge, architect, artisan, all those who once crowded the city-streets have alike disappeared from the cities. No one now ever brings in goods for the market. There is no one to buy them or sell them. Only a century ago men still bought and sold goods in exchange for coined money. But ever since then exchange by barter has been the sole practice. Coins no longer circulate.

The great collapse had taken place less than a century previously; yet no one could now explain what it was which had happened or how it had happened. Men's knowledge of their history, their own history, had evaporated. Of the four hundred years of the Roman occupation of Britain men

---

[106] Synesius, *Catastasis*, II.3.
[107] Gildas, *De Excidio*, I.3,2.

knew now of little more than that kings across the sea had once ruled the island. Their governors had been harsh. There had been a Great Persecution of christians and a ruler called Magnus Maximus. And that was practically all. If we may generalise from the case of Gildas, an educated man, Britons in that part of the island not yet invaded by the Saxons knew little of the part which the invaders had now occupied. They knew that they could no longer visit Verulamium or Caerleon, both of which were in the intruders' hands.[108] They knew that merchants no longer brought luxury goods from abroad up the Thames or the Severn.[109] Gildas – if we may judge by what he tells us or omits to tell us – knew nothing of Germanus of Auxerre (who had visited a distant part of the island) or of Constantius's *Life* of him and little of the Roman empire itself, its past or its present; he knew nothing of Armorica to which so many of his compatriots had already fled and were still flying, and he never mentions it. On the other hand, he never mentions Ireland, and yet it is hard to believe that he was wholly ignorant of it, for there was much coming and going across the Irish Sea in his day.[110] And he is aware that if you cross the Channel from Britain you reach Gallia Belgica, that is (although he may not have known it) the province in which Boulogne lay; and Boulogne for centuries had been the regular Continental port for Britain. As far as we can discover, Gildas knew nothing whatever, apart from this handful of facts, about the Roman empire as a whole or about the past history of the entire world.[111] The most frightening feature in the picture drawn by Gildas is not the destruction of city-life in Britain or the break-up of the Imperial system with its guarantee of peaceful life, but rather the destruction of knowledge itself. Knowledge of the outside world and knowledge of the past had been wiped out of men's minds.

[108] Caerleon may not yet have been held permanently by them. As Jackson, *Language and History*, p. 17, remarks: 'at any given stage the invaders may easily have raided far outside the areas which they had permanently occupied and settled'.
[109] Gildas, *De Excidio*, I.3,1.
[110] See, for example, Hughes, *The Church*, p. 49, *et passim*.
[111] Several of these assertions are justified in Thompson, 'Gildas'.

Bibliography

ALCOCK, Leslie *Arthur's Britain. History and Archaeology, A.D. 367–634* (2nd edn, Harmondsworth 1973)

ANDERSON, W. B. (ed. & transl.) *Sidonius: Poems and Letters* (2 vols, Cambridge, Mass. 1936–65)

AUSTIN, N. J. E. *Ammianus on Warfare: an Investigation into Ammianus' Military Knowledge* (Brussels 1979)

BACHRACH, Bernard S. *A History of the Alans in the West from their First Appearance in the Sources of Classical Antiquity through the Early Middle Ages* (Minneapolis, Minn. 1973)

BARDY, G. 'Constance de Lyon, biographe de saint Germain d'Auxerre', in *Saint Germain*, pp. 89–108

BARLEY, M. W. & HANSON, R. P. C. (edd.) *Christianity in Britain, 300–700* (Leicester 1968)

BARNES, T. D. 'Merobaudes on the Imperial family', *Phoenix* 28 (1974) 314–19

BARNES, T. D. '*Patricii* under Valentinian III', *Phoenix* 29 (1975) 155–70

BARTHOLOMEW, P. 'Fifth-century facts', *Britannia* 13 (1982) 261–70

BENOIT, F. 'L'hilarianum d'Arles et les missions en Bretagne (Ve–VIe siècles)', in *Saint Germain*, pp. 181–9

BINCHY, D. A. 'Patrick and his biographers, ancient and modern', *Studia Hibernica* 2 (1962) 7–173

BISCHOFF, B. & KOEHLER, W. 'Eine illustrierte Ausgabe der spätantiken Ravennater Annalen', in *Medieval Studies in Memory of A. Kingsley Porter*, ed. W. R. W. Koehler (2 vols, Cambridge, Mass. 1939), I.125–38

BLOCKLEY, R. C. *Ammianus Marcellinus: a Study of his Historiography and Political Thought* (Brussels 1975)

BLOCKLEY, R. C. 'The date of the "barbarian conspiracy"', *Britannia* 11 (1980) 223–5

BORIUS, René (ed. & transl.) *Constance de Lyon: Vie de saint Germain d'Auxerre* (Paris 1965)

BROWN, Peter 'Pelagius and his supporters: aims and environment', *Journal of Theological Studies*, N.S., 19 (1968) 93–114, reprinted in his *Religion and Society in the Age of Saint Augustine* (London 1972), pp. 183–207

BURY, J. B.   *History of the Later Roman Empire from the Death of Theodosius I. to the Death of Justinian (A.D. 395 to A.D. 565)* (2 vols, London 1923)

CAMERON, K.   'Eccles in English place-names', in *Christianity in Britain, 300–700*, edd. M. W. Barley & R. P. C. Hanson (Leicester 1968), pp. 87–92.

CAMERON, K.   'The meaning and significance of Old English *walh* in English place-names', *Journal of the English Place-name Society* 12 (1979/80) 1–53

CASEY, P. J.   'Magnus Maximus in Britain', in *The End of Roman Britain*, ed. P. J. Casey (Oxford 1979), pp. 66–79

CASEY, P. J. (ed.)   *The End of Roman Britain* (Oxford 1979)

CAVALLIN, Samuel (ed.)   *Vitae sanctorum Honorati et Hilarii episcoporum Arelatensium* (Lund 1952)

CHADWICK, H. M.   *The Origin of the English Nation* (Cambridge 1907)

CHADWICK, N. K.   'Intellectual contacts between Britain and Gaul in the fifth century', in *Studies in Early British History*, ed. N. K. Chadwick (Cambridge 1954; rev. imp., 1959), pp. 189–263

CHADWICK, Nora K.   *Poetry and Letters in Early Christian Gaul* (London 1955)

CHADWICK, Nora K. (ed.)   *Studies in Early British History* (Cambridge 1954; rev. imp., 1959)

CLAUDE, D.   'Die Handwerker der Merowingerzeit nach den erzählenden und urkundlichen Quellen', *Abhandlungen der Akademie der Wissenschaften in Göttingen, phil.-hist. Klasse* (1981) 204–66

CLOVER, Frank M. (transl.)   *Flavius Merobaudes: a Translation and Historical Commentary* (Philadelphia, Pa. 1971)

COLLINGWOOD, R. G. & MYRES, J. N. L.   *Roman Britain and the English Settlements* (2nd edn, Oxford 1937)

COURTOIS, Christian   *Les Vandales et l'Afrique* (Paris 1955)

DAICHES, David & THORLBY, A. (edd.)   *Literature and Western Civilization, II, The Mediaeval World* (London 1973)

DELEHAYE, Hippolyte   *Les légendes hagiographiques* (4th edn, Brussels 1955)

DEMOUGEOT, E.   'Les invasions germaniques et la rupture des relations entre la Bretagne et la Gaule', *Le moyen âge*, 68 [4th S., 17] (1962) 1–50

DE PLINVAL, G.   'Les campagnes de saint Germain en Grande-Bretagne contre les Pélagiens', in *Saint Germain*, pp. 135–49

DE PLINVAL, Georges   *Pélage: ses écrits, sa vie et sa réforme. Étude d'histoire littéraire et religieuse* (Lausanne 1943)

DE STE. CROIX, G. E. M.   *The Class Struggle in the Ancient Greek World from the Archaic Age to the Arab Conquests* (London 1981)

DESSAU, Hermann (ed.)   *Inscriptiones latinae selectae* (3 vols in 5, Berlin 1892–1916)

DICKINSON, T. M.   'British antiquity: post-Roman and pagan Anglo-Saxon', *Archaeological Journal* 134 (1977) 404–18

DIEHL, Ernst (ed.)   *Inscriptiones latinae christianae ueteres* (3 vols, Berlin 1925–31; suppl., Dublin & Zürich 1967)

DOBLHOFER, Ernst (ed.) *Rutilius Claudius Namatianus: De reditu suo sive Iter gallicum* (2 vols, Heidelberg 1972–7)

DUCHESNE, L. *Fastes épiscopaux de l'ancienne Gaule* (3 vols, Paris 1894–1915)

DUMVILLE, D. N. 'Kingship, genealogies and regnal lists', in *Early Medieval Kingship*, edd. P. H. Sawyer & I. N. Wood (Leeds 1977), pp. 72–104

DUMVILLE, D. N. 'Sub-Roman Britain: history and legend', *History*, N.S., 62 (1977) 173–92

ENSSLIN, W. 'Zum Heermeisteramt des spätrömischen Reiches: III. Der magister utriusque militiae et patricius des 5. Jahrhunderts', *Klio* 24 [N.F., 6] (1930/1) 467–502

EVANS, J. 'S. Germanus in Britain', *Archaeologia Cantiana* 80 (1965) 175–85

FINLEY, M. I. (ed.) *Slavery in Classical Antiquity: Views and Controversies* (Cambridge 1960)

FRANSES, D. *Paus Leo de Groote en S. Hilarius van Arles* ('s Hertogenbosch 1948)

FREND, W. H. C. 'The christianization of Roman Britain', in *Christianity in Britain, 300–700*, edd. M. W. Barley & R. P. C. Hanson (Leicester 1968), pp. 37–49.

FRERE, Sheppard *Britannia. A History of Roman Britain* (2nd edn, London 1974)

FULFORD, M. 'Pottery production and trade at the end of Roman Britain: the case against continuity', in *The End of Roman Britain*, ed. P. J. Casey (Oxford 1979), pp. 120–32

GADD, C. J. *Ideas of Divine Rule in the Ancient East* (London 1948)

GAUDEMET, J. 'La carrière civile de saint Germain', in *Saint Germain*, pp. 111–18

GELLING, Margaret *Signposts to the Past. Place-names and the History of England* (London 1978)

GESSEL, W. 'Germanus von Auxerre (um 378 bis 448). Die Vita des Konstantius von Lyon als homiletische Paränese in hagiographischer Form', *Römische Quartalschrift für christliche Altertumskunde und Kirchengeschichte* 65 (1970) 1–14

GILLAM, J. 'Romano-Saxon pottery: an alternative interpretation', in *The End of Roman Britain*, ed. P. J. Casey (Oxford 1979), pp. 103–18

GOODBURN, R. & BARTHOLOMEW, P. (edd.) *Aspects of the* Notitia Dignitatum (Oxford 1976)

GRIMES, W. F. (ed.) *Aspects of Archaeology in Britain and Beyond. Essays presented to O. G. S. Crawford* (London 1951)

GROSJEAN, P. 'Notes d'hagiographie celtique, 27–36', *Analecta Bollandiana* 75 (1957) 160–226

HANSON, R. P. C. *Saint Patrick, His Origins and Career* (Oxford 1968)

HANSON, R. P. C. 'The Church in fifth-century Gaul: evidence from Sidonius Apollinaris', *Journal of Ecclesiastical History* 21 (1970) 1–10

HANSON, R. P. C.   'The date of St. Patrick', *Bulletin of the John Rylands University Library of Manchester* 61 (1978/9) 60–77

HANSON, W. S. & KEPPIE, L. J. F. (edd.)   *Roman Frontier Studies 1979. Papers presented to the 12th International Congress of Roman Frontier Studies* (3 vols, Oxford 1980)

HIND, J. G. F.   'Litus saxonicum – the meaning of "Saxon Shore" ', in *Roman Frontier Studies 1979*, edd. W. S. Hanson & L. J. F. Keppie (3 vols, Oxford 1980), I.317–24

HOARE, F. R. (transl.)   *The Western Fathers* (London 1954)

HODGKIN, R. H.   *A History of the Anglo-Saxons* (3rd edn, 2 vols, London 1952)

HOFMANN, J. B.   *Lateinische Syntax und Stilistik*, revised by A. Szantyr (Munich 1965)

HOGG, A. H. A.   'The survival of Romano-British place-names in southern Britain', *Antiquity* 38 (1964) 296–9

HUGHES, Kathleen   *The Church in Early Irish Society* (London 1966)

JACKSON, K.   'The British languages and their evolution', in *Literature and Western Civilization*, II, *The Mediaeval World*, edd. D. Daiches & A. Thorlby (London 1973), pp. 113–26

JACKSON, Kenneth   *Language and History in Early Britain. A Chronological Survey of the Brittonic Languages, 1st to 12th c. A.D.* (Edinburgh 1953)

JACKSON, K.   'The British language during the period of the English settlements', in *Studies in Early British History*, ed. N. K. Chadwick (Cambridge 1954; rev. imp., 1959), pp. 61–82

JOHNSON, S.   'Channel commands in the Notitia', in *Aspects of the* Notitia Dignitatum, edd. R. Goodburn & P. Bartholomew (Oxford 1976), pp. 81–102

JOHNSON, Stephen   *Later Roman Britain* (London 1980)

JONES, A. H. M.   *The Greek City from Alexander to Justinian* (Oxford 1940)

JONES, A. H. M.   *The Later Roman Empire, 284–602. A Social, Economic, and Administrative Survey* (4 vols, Oxford 1964)

JONES, A. H. M., *et al.*   *The Prosopography of the Later Roman Empire*, vols I–II (Cambridge 1971, 1980)

KOEHLER, Wilhelm R. W. (ed.)   *Medieval Studies in Memory of A. Kingsley Porter* (2 vols, Cambridge, Mass. 1939)

KOLON, Benedikt (ed.)   *Die Vita S. Hilarii Arelatensis. Eine eidographische Studie* (Paderborn 1925)

KRUSCH, Bruno (ed.)   *Passiones vitaeque sanctorum aevi merovingici et antiquorum aliquot*, volume III (Hannover 1896)

KRUSCH, Bruno & LEVISON, W. (edd.)   *Passiones vitaeque sanctorum aevi merovingici*, volume VII (Hannover 1919–20)

LANGGÄRTNER, Georg   *Die Gallienpolitik der Päpste im 5. und 6. Jahrhundert. Eine Studie über den apostolischen Vikariat von Arles* (Bonn 1964)

LEVISON, W.   'Bischof Germanus von Auxerre und die Quellen zu seiner Geschichte', *Neues Archiv der Gesellschaft für ältere deutsche Geschichtskunde* 29 (1903/4) 95–175

LEVISON, W. 'St. Alban and St. Alban's', *Antiquity* 15 (1941) 337–59

LOT, F. 'Bretons et anglais aux Ve et VIe siècles', *Proceedings of the British Academy* 16 (1930) 327–44

LOYEN, A. 'L'oeuvre de Flavius Merobaudes et l'histoire de l'Occident de 430 à 450', *Revue des études anciennes* 74 (1972) 153–74

MANSI, J.-D. (ed.) *Sacrorum conciliorum nova et amplissima collectio* (53 vols, Paris 1759–98)

MARROU, H. I. 'Le dossier épigraphique de l'évêque Rusticus de Narbonne', *Rivista di archeologia cristiana* 46 (1970) 331–49

MATHISEN, R. W. 'Hilarius, Germanus, and Lupus: the aristocratic background of the Chelidonius affair', *Phoenix* 33 (1979) 160–9

MATHISEN, R. W. 'The last year of saint Germanus of Auxerre', *Analecta Bollandiana* 99 (1981) 151–9

MESLIN, M. [review of Borius, *Constance*], *Revue de l'histoire des religions* 170 (1966) 204–7

MIGNE, J.-P. (ed.) *Patrologiae [latinae] cursus completus . . .* (221 vols, Paris 1844–64)

MILLER, M. 'Bede's use of Gildas', *English Historical Review* 90 (1975) 241–61

MILLER, M. 'The last British entry in the "Gallic Chronicles" ', *Britannia* 9 (1978) 315–18

MOMMSEN, Theodor (ed.) *Chronica minora saec. IV.V.VI.VII.* (3 vols, Berlin 1891–8)

MOMMSEN, Theodor *Gesammelte Schriften*, volume VII (Berlin 1909)

MUTZENBECHER, Almut (ed.) *Maximi Episcopi Taurinensis collectionem sermonum antiquam nonnullis sermonibus extrauagantibus adiectis* (Turnhout 1962)

MYRES, J. N. L. 'Pelagius and the end of Roman rule in Britain', *Journal of Roman Studies* 50 (1960) 21–36

MYRES, J. N. L. 'The Adventus Saxonum', in *Aspects of Archaeology in Britain and Beyond. Essays presented to O. G. S. Crawford*, ed. W. F. Grimes (London 1951), pp. 221–41

OOST, Stewart Irvin *Galla Placidia Augusta: a Biographical Essay* (Chicago, Ill. 1968)

O'SULLIVAN, Thomas D. *The De Excidio of Gildas, its Authenticity and Date* (Leiden 1978)

PAULY'S *Realencyclopädie der classischen Altertumswissenschaft*, ed. G. Wissowa (Stuttgart 1894–in progress)

PELTERET, D. 'Slave raiding and slave trading in early England', *Anglo-Saxon England* 9 (1981) 99–114

RIVET, A. L. F. (ed.) *The Roman Villa in Britain* (London 1969)

RIVET, A. L. F. & SMITH, C. *The Place-names of Roman Britain* (London 1979)

ROBERTS, William I. *Romano-Saxon Pottery* (Oxford 1982)

ROLFE, John C. (ed. & transl.) *Ammianus Marcellinus* (3 vols, Cambridge, Mass. 1935–40)

ROWLEY, Trevor (ed.) *Anglo-Saxon Settlement and Landscape* (Oxford 1974)

Saint Germain d'Auxerre et son temps: Communications présentées à l'occasion du XIXe *Congrès de l'Association Bourguignonne des Sociétés Savantes réuni à Auxerre (29 juillet–2 août 1948)*, with an introduction by Gabriel Le Bras (Auxerre 1950)

SAWYER, P. H. & WOOD, I. N. (edd.)   *Early Medieval Kingship* (Leeds 1977)

SCHMIDT, L.   *Geschichte der deutschen Stämme bis zum Ausgang der Völkerwanderung* (2nd edn, 3 vols, Munich 1940)

SEECK, Otto   *Geschichte des Untergangs der antiken Welt* (6 vols in 12, Berlin 1895–1913 *and* Stuttgart 1920–1)

STEIN, E.   'Beiträge zur Geschichte von Ravenna in spätrömischer und byzantinischer Zeit', *Klio* 16 (1919/20) 40–71

STEIN, E.   *Histoire du bas-empire* (2 vols, Paris 1959/49)

STENTON, F. M.   *Anglo-Saxon England* (3rd edn, Oxford 1971)

STEVENS, C. E.   'Marcus, Gratian, Constantine', *Athenaeum* [Pavia] 45 [N.S., 35] (1957) 316–47

STEVENS, C. E.   *Sidonius Apollinaris and his Age* (Oxford 1933)

SVENNUNG, J.   *Untersuchungen zu Palladius und zur lateinischen Fach- und Volkssprache* (Uppsala 1935)

SWANTON, M. J.   *The Spearheads of the Anglo-Saxon Settlements* (London 1973)

TAYLOR, C.   'The Anglo-Saxon countryside', in *Anglo-Saxon Settlement and Landscape*, ed. T. Rowley (Oxford 1974), pp. 5–15

THOMAS, Charles   *Christianity in Roman Britain to A.D. 500* (London 1981)

THOMPSON, E. A.   'A chronological note on St. Germanus of Auxerre', *Analecta Bollandiana* 75 (1957) 135–8

THOMPSON, E. A.   'Barbarian invaders and Roman collaborators', *Florilegium* [Ottawa] 2 (1980) 71–88

THOMPSON, E. A.   'Britain, A.D. 406–410', *Britannia* 8 (1977) 303–18

THOMPSON, E. A.   'Gildas and the history of Britain', *Britannia* 10 (1979) 203–26 *and* 11 (1980) 344.

THOMPSON, E. A.   'Procopius on Brittia and Britannia', *Classical Quarterly* 74 [N.S., 30] (1980) 498–507

THOMPSON, E. A.   *Romans and Barbarians. The Decline of the Western Empire* (Madison, Wisc. 1982)

THOMPSON, E. A.   'Slavery in early Germany', *Hermathena* 89 (1957) 17–29, reprinted in *Slavery in Classical Antiquity*, ed. M. I. Finley (Cambridge 1960), pp. 191–203

THOMPSON, E. A.   *The Early Germans* (Oxford 1965; rev. imp., 1968)

THOMPSON, E. A.   'Zosimus, 6.10.2, and the letters of Honorius', *Classical Quarterly* 76 [N.S., 32] (1982) 445–62

TODD, Malcolm   *Roman Britain, 55 B.C.–A.D. 400. The Province beyond Ocean* (Brighton 1981)

TODD, Malcolm (ed.)   *Studies in the Romano-British Villa* (Leicester 1978)

TOMLIN, R.   'The date of the "barbarian conspiracy"', *Britannia* 5 (1974) 303–9

VON HARTEL, Wilhelm (ed.)   *Magni Felicis Ennodii opera omnia* (Wien 1882)

WACHER, John   *The Towns of Roman Britain* (London 1974)

WHITELOCK, Dorothy (transl.)   *English Historical Documents* c. *500–1042* (2nd edn, London 1979)

WILLIAMS, Hugh   *Christianity in Early Britain* (Oxford 1912)

WILLIAMS, Hugh (ed. & transl.)   *Gildas* (2 vols, London 1899–1901)

WINTERBOTTOM, Michael (ed. & transl.)   *Gildas: The Ruin of Britain and Other Works* (Chichester 1978)

Index

Acolius, 68

Adouacrius, 95 n. 14

Aetius, Hallelujah battle and, 46; patrician, 60f.; Armorica and, 62; Burgundians and, 62, 65; Alans and, 64, 72, 74; consul iii, 65; Britons appeal to, 92; absent from Ravenna, 74; ignored by Germanus, 74f.; plans wrecked by Germanus, 75

Africa, 29, 101, 111

Agrestius, 78

Agricola, Flavian general, 22

Agricola, Pelagian, 21f., 25, 31, 54, 81

Alamanni, 97f., 103f., 109

Alans, 62f.; invade Gaul, 35 n. 42, 98; ordered to crush Armoricans, 62, 72; nomads, 64, 72; settled near Orléans, 64. See also Goar.

Alaric, 94

Alban, St Albans, 4, 49, 50, 55, 81

Albinus, 59 n. 18

Alesia, Alise-Sainte-Reine, 8, 78

Alps, 73

Amida, 105

Ammianus Marcellinus, on conspiracy of 367, 44 with n. 27, 52 n. 38, 53 n. 41, 105 n. 70, 108 n. 85; on Alamanni, 109

Angers, 95 n. 14

Anglesey, 101

Annianus, 86

annonae, 97

Antioch, 44 n. 27

Antonine Itinerary, 50

Antoninus of Merida, 28 n. 9

Aquitanica Secunda, 71, 97, 111

Arinthaeus, 61

Arles, 8, 67; Germanus in, 2, 58f., 78; alleged synod of, 79 n. 8. See also Caesarius, Hilary, Ravennius.

Armorica, Armoricans, composed of *prouinciae*, 9 n. 11; extent of, 35, 71; revolt of, 1; secede from Roman empire, 35f., 72, 76; suppressed in 417, 36; not harried by Saxons, 35 n. 42, 44; date of revolt of, 56 n. 8, 61f., 63f., 70; reasons for revolt, 72; peace in, 65; appeal to Germanus, 61, 65f., 71f., 75f., 77; renew revolt, 75f.;

Constantius's attitude to, 89, cf. 71f., 77; Visigoths and, 97; apparently unknown to Gildas, 115

Arthur, King, 95

Aruandus, 102

Astigi, 60

Astorga, 102, 107

Asturis, 103

Attacotti, 44, 53

Attila, 86

Augustine of Canterbury, 91

Augustine of Hippo, 21

Augustus, 73

Austria, 2

Austurians, 114

Autun, 8, 88, 89

Auvergne, 62

Auxerre, mentioned, 7, 8, 65, 81; alleged visit of St Patrick to, 5; *plebs* and *populus* of, 8; pagans near, 16; road to Boulogne from, 51 n. 35; taxes of, 66f.; in Armorica, 71; paganism near, 88

Auxiliaris, 2, 58f., 66f., 78, 87

Avignon, 58

Avitus, Eparchius, 67

Bacaudae, 34, 62f., 104 n. 65

Badon, Mount, 100

ballistae, 107

Baptism, 18

Barbarian Conspiracy of 367, 44, 52 n. 38, 93, 105 n. 70. See Ammianus.

Batavis, 103

Bede, on Severus, 4 n. 10, 23; and St Patrick, 5; accused of prejudice, 20 n. 25; on chronology, 91f.; on British attitude to Saxons, 113

Belgica Secunda, 51 n. 35

Besançon: see Celidonius.

Boulogne, 51 with n. 35, 52, 92, 115

Braga, 107

Britain, Britons, second visit of Germanus to, 4, 28f., 47f., 54, 79, 84; date of, 1, 56f.; unity of destroyed, 37; first visit to by Germanus, 5, 16–20, 24f., 28, 48, 50, 56; cause of, 25, 79f.; alternative dating of, 56;

123

Britain, Britons (*contd.*)
  political indifference to visiting bishops,
  28f.; city-life in, 9f., 13, 17; tyrants in, 12,
  100; lack of information about, 13f., 85;
  paganism in, 15, 19; perhaps pagan rule
  in, 32f.; languages of, 15, 16 n. 4, 18;
  churches in, 9, 16f.; religion in, 15, 24;
  bishops of, 19f., 22f., 81; their need of
  urgent help, 24f.; Pelagianism in, 19–23;
  Roman law in, 29, 32; Pelagian success,
  31; rebellion of in 409, 32f., 72; secede
  from Roman empire, 32, 34f., 72, 76;
  Bacaudae in, 34; fail to pursue enemy, 42;
  skilful reconnaissance of, 41; survival of,
  53; imitated by Armoricans, 72; alleged
  orthodoxy in Constantius's time, 84f.;
  famines in, 99; civil wars among, 99f.,
  110; cities of, 101–4, 106, 108, 110; flight
  of, 103; slaves, 114
Brittany, 71
Burgundians, 62, 65, 74, 97; federates in
  Gaul, 110f.
Byzantium, 100

Caelestius, 19 n. 20
Caerleon, 115 with n. 108
Caerwent, 108
Caesarius of Arles, 24
Caistor-by-Norwich, 108
Caledonia, 45 n. 28, 48
campestris, 16f.
cancellarius, 13, 60 with n. 26
Candida Casa, 48
Canterbury, 52
Carausius, 93
Carthage, Council of, 21f.; fall of, 102
Cassiodorus, 78 n. 3
Celestine I, Pope, 24, 29f., 31, 79f.
Celidonius, 56f., 58f., 61, 86
Celtic language in Britain, 15, 16 n. 1, 110,
  113
Celtic names among Saxons, 95f., 114
Chartres, 71
Chelidonius: see Celidonius.
Chichester, 50f.
Chronicle of A.D. 452: see Gallic. . . .
Churches in Britain, 9, 16f.
Cirencester, 51, 53, 108
City-life in Britain, 9f., 101–4, 106, 108, 110
ciues, 8, 9
ciuitas, 8, 9, 13, 51, 76
Clermont Ferrand, 103 n. 64
colonia in Gildas, 106 with n. 77, 107
Conimbrica, 107
Constantine the Great, 10
Constantine III, 21, 32, 35, 51
Constantinople, 68f.
Constantius of Lyon, contents of *Vita*, 1;
  date of, 1 n. 1; on Germanus's second visit
  to Britain, 2, 4, 12, 14, 23, 28, 47f., 79f.; on
  chronology, 3, 23, 67; and Lupus of

Troyes, 3; value of, 4, 79f.; on Severus, 4;
  purpose of *Vita*, 2, 20, 24, 75, 85f.; on
  Germanus's first visit to Britain, 5, 14–16,
  20, 24f., 48, 50, 79f., 81; age of, 82; silence
  of, 5, 74f., 79; on religion, 15, 17; apparent
  ignorance of Pelagianism, 24, 81; on man
  of tribunician power, 6, 11, 26; on
  Sigisvult, 60f.; on British legation, 7, 79;
  less reliable than Prosper, 6, 8, 14, 29f.,
  79f., 84; on miracles, 87f.; use of *populus*
  and *plebs*, 8; proper names in, 11; on
  geography, 13; lack of information about
  Britain, 13, 20, 23, 79f.; and about pope,
  30, 80; and about Agricola, 81; mentions
  interpreter, 16, 18; on city-life in Britain,
  9f., 13, 17; on Ravenna, 20f.; on Peter
  Chrysologus, 20f.; silent on British Church-
  organisation, 23; on Gaul and Italy, 8–11,
  23, 73; perhaps a cleric, 24, 78; use of
  inscia, 47 n. 5; and of *turba, multitudo*, 51;
  on Hallelujah victory, 39, 40f.; on visit to
  Verulamium, 49, 81; on Hilary of Arles,
  58, 78; on Armoricans, 62–5, 71f., 77; use
  of *uel*, 73f.; on Aetius, 73; on Lyon, 78f.; on
  Lupus, 82; Italian authorities of, 83; on
  Germanus's early career, 83, 86f.; on contemporary Britain, 84f., 114; writes for
  rich readers, 89; unknown to Gildas, 115.
  See also Elafius.
Constantius, patrician, 97, 111
Constantius of Uzès, 58f.
'Continuity', 97, 110
Couiacense castrum, 102
curia, 106
curiales, 33
Cyrenaica, 114

Danube, River, 97; Germans on, 11f.
Denmark, 46
Deserters from the army, 35
Devon, 101
Dicaledones, 44
Diocletian, 106 n. 77
districtio, 87 n. 42
Dorchester, 50, 54, 98
Dover, 52
dux Tractus Armoricani, 62 n. 29, 71, 83

Ecija: see Astigi.
Edwin, King, 92
Egyptians, 94 n. 13
Elafius, 4, 9; *primus*, 12, 26f.; mentioned, 23,
  24, 28, 47, 84
English Channel, 4f., 56
Eudoxia, 68, 69f.
Eudoxius, 35
euectio, 10 with n. 41, 69
Eugippius, 1, 2f., 73 n. 13, 99
Exuperantius, 36, 72

Famine, 98f.
Federates, 91, 98 n. 30, 111
Franks, 44 with n. 27, 46 n. 22, 52 n. 35, 104

Galla Placidia: see Placidia.
Gallaecia, 112f.
Gallia Belgica, 115
Gallic Chronicle of A.D. 452, silent on raid
   of 429, 43f.; on 440s in Britain, 44, 47 with
   n. 2; accuracy of, 61; on Tibatto, 62, 63,
   65, 89; on Germanus, 62 n. 29, 87; on
   Alans, 64; on Armorica, 72; on aims of
   Armoricans, 72; on Saxon domination,
   91f.
Garonne, 71
Gaul, Gauls, called *plebs*, 8; communications
   in, 10, 11 n. 49; *rex* in, 12; Pelagians
   banished to and from, 31; alleged synod
   in, 31, 79; possible return of Pelagianism
   to, 50; taxes of, 66f.; christian or pagan?
   88; invaded by Alamanni, 98, 104;
   Visigoths and Burgundians in, 110f.
Germany, 44f.
Gesta de purgatione Xysti, 60 n. 26
Gildas, on British clergy, 17, 20; does not
   mention Pelagianism, 22f. 31; on fifth-
   century Britain, 37, 99; on British kings,
   37, 101; on the Picts, 45; a metaphor of,
   50; on Saxon Federates, 91; on 'proud
   tyrant', 92; on famines, 98; on flight of
   Britons, 103; on fall of cities, 105f.; on
   empty cities, 107, 110; silent on villas,
   105; on contemporary Britain, 114f.;
   ignorant of Constantius's *Vita*, 115; silent
   about Ireland, 115. See also Proud
   tyrant; *colonia*.
Gironde, 97
Goar, addressed through interpreter, 16, 19;
   ordered to suppress Armoricans, 62, 65,
   72; settled near Orléans, 64; fate of
   unknown, 71; requires amnesty for
   Armoricans, 73; disobeys orders, 75;
   pagan, 88
Goths, 33, 62. See also Visigoths.
Gratian, Emperor, 30 n. 17
Gratian, usurper, 35
Gregory the Great, 92

Hadrian's Wall, 105, 107
Hagiography and chronology, 2f.
Hallelujah victory, 2, 39–46; no pursuit
   after, 42; site of, 52
Hengist, 95
Heruls, 46
Hilary of Arles, 56f., 58, 78, 86
Honorius, law of, 19 n. 20, 28f., cf. 32; letters
   of, 32 n. 27, 37, 76; mentioned, 35
Horsa, 95
hospitalitas, 64 n. 42
Huns, 35, 71, 74, 97
Hydatius, 102, 107

Ianuarius, 10, 83
Icklingham, 17 n. 10
incruenta, 107, 112
interea, 68 with n. 64
Ioviaco, 103
Ireland, Irish, 44, 53, 81, 94, 98f., 101;
   unfamiliar to Gildas, 115. See Palladius;
   Scotti.
Italians, called *populus*, not *plebs*, 8
Italy, 8, 11. See also Milan, Placentia,
   Ravenna, Rome, Turin.

Julian Caesar, 105
Julius Caesar, 94

Kent, 52f.
Köln, 109 n. 90

Latin language, 15, 18, 110, 113
Leo I, Pope, 25, 56f., 58f.
Leporius, 11, 88, 89
Lincoln, 53 with n. 42, 54
Lisbon, 102f.
Litorius, 62, 71
Loire, River, 71, 97
London, 50f.; possible scene of debate, 53,
   81
Lugdunensis Senonia, 10, 71
Lupus of Troyes, 3, 19, 55, 79f., 81, 82 with
   n. 16; praised by Sidonius, 86
Lusidius, 102f.
Lusitania, 28 n. 9, 107
Lyon, 7, 8; Constantius of, 78; Germanus in,
   78f., 81, 84

Magnentius, 104
Magnus Maximus, 10, 115
Main, River, 109
maiores personae, 11
Manichaeans, 28 n. 9
Marcellinus, 61
Marcian, 91
Marcomanni, 97
Maroboduus, 94 n. 13
Marseilles, 67
Martylum, 102
Maximus of Turin, 16
Mayo, County, 46
mediocres personae, 11, 87
Medway, River, 52
Merida, 28 n. 9, 102
Merobaudes, 61, 65
Mesopotamia, 105
Milan, 8, 55, 65f., 86f., 88
Miracles, 87
Moors, 12

Narbonne, 56 n. 9, 62
Nectariola, 78
Nectarius, 58f.

125

127

DATE DUE

HIGHSMITH   # 45220